Essential Maths

3

Jayashri Bhattacharya

Preface

Mathematics has always been an integral part of human life. From times immemorial, Mathematics has been in our everyday life in various ways irrespective of our knowledge of the mathematical concepts involved in various activities. The school curriculum focuses on the mathematical concepts to cultivate thinking and developing the reasoning skills. It enables the students to take up a systematic approach to solve their daily life problems, aims at exploring multiple aspects of the subject and thus develop a passion for it.

Essential Maths is a series that strives to focus on the maximum involvement of children following an interactive learning pattern. It has been authored by a senior teacher who has been dedicating her years to the teaching of this subject. Following this series will help students to keep away from rote learning and develop their confidence. Their increased confidence and flexibility with numbers willhelp them handle abstractions and develop logical approach towards the subject. The review exercises help the learners assess their understanding of the concepts. This series also develops the potential of the learners for continuous and comprehensive evaluation, by inculcating the scholastics and co-scholastic skills. Its activity based interactive style will sharpen the learners' minds and make learning enriching and joyous. The books are beautifully illustrated which adds to the overall appeal of the series.

From the Author

Mathematics has always been an integral part of human life. We use mathematics in our everyday life in various ways without being aware of our knowledge of the mathematical concepts involved in the activity. School curriculum includes the study of Mathematics in order to focus on mathematical concepts which help to cultivate the thinking and reasoning skills. It is a systematic approach to enable students to solve their daily life problems. It also aims to allow the students to explore the multiple aspects of the subject and develop a passion for it.

The lab activities and exercises can be used by the teachers as a demonstrative toolin the Maths Lab.

Objectives of teaching Mathematics are:

- To develop an ability to think and reason mathematically
- To handle abstractions
- To cultivate a positive attitude towards mathematics following an interactive learning pattern to help the teacher ensure maximum involvement of the learners
- To increase confidence and flexibility of the learners when numbers are concerned
- To discourage rote learning
- To develop logical sense along with a passion for the subject

The series **Essential Maths** is a carefully graded series prepared in accordance with the new syllabus prescribed by the NCERT on the basis of CCE (Continuous and Comprehensive Evaluation). A remarkable feature of this series is that all the exercises are formed in such a manner that they begin with easy exercises and gradually progresses to difficult ones. The books are activity based and extensive drilling with integrated revision exercises form its key feature. All the books are fullof colourful illustrations which make learning a joy! They also inculcate scholastic and co-scholastic skills in the learner.

I take this opportunity to thank a few people who have helped me write this series. They are Ms Seema Chawla my editor for continuously guiding me, my friend Ms Tapasi (Managing Editor, B Jain), my parents-in-law for encouraging me and Aurobindo, my husband, for being very supportive. Heartfelt thanks to Sofia and Shantanu, my kids. Without their suggestions and criticism, I would not have been able to undertake and complete this project.

Jayashri Bhattacharya

Contents

1. Revision 5

2. Numbers (Up to Ten Thousand) 10

3. Addition of 4-Digit Numbers 27

4. Subtraction 35

5. Multiplication 43

6. Division 61

7. Fractions 75

8. Time 83

9. Symmetry and Patterns 95

10. Money 99

11. Measurement of Length 105

12. Measurement of Mass 110

13. Measurement of Capacity 115

14. Geometry 121

15. Data-Handling 127

16. Review Exercise 1, 2, 3, 4 130

17. Answers 138

Revision

1. Colour the given figure as instructed.

100-125 Red

200-250 Grey

300-370 Black

400-500 Blue

700-800 Pink

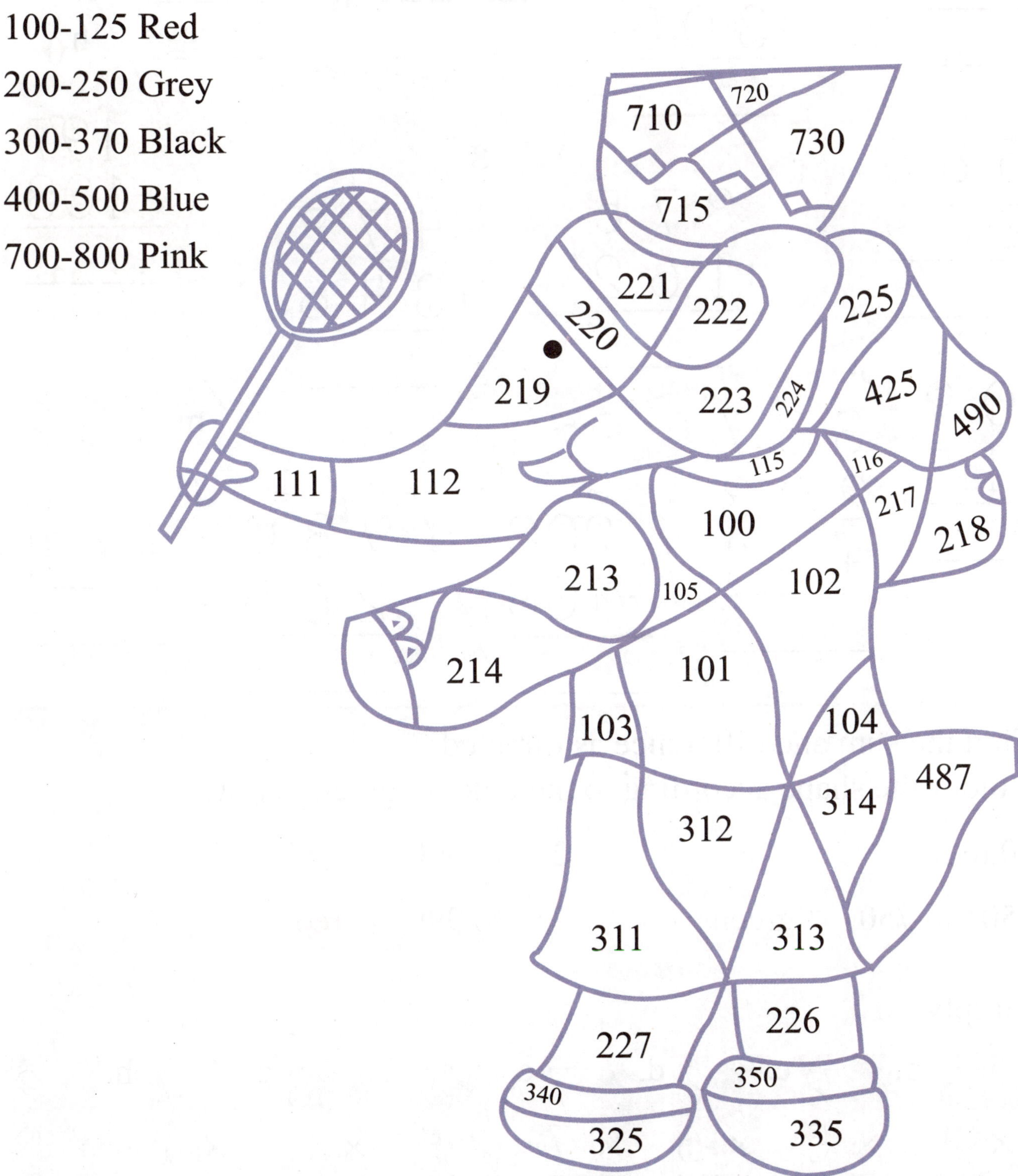

2. Let us add and subtract 3-digit numbers.

a.
```
  3 6
+ 2 1
-----
```

b.
```
  1 0 0
    9 5
+ 3 0 5
-------
```

c.
```
  3 0 0
+ 2 0 0
-------
```

d.
```
  2 2 2
+ 3 3 3
-------
```

e.
```
  5 8 6
+ 2 0 9
-------
```

f.
```
  3 7 5
+ 1 6 2
-------
```

g.
```
  4 7 8
+ 3 4 6
-------
```

h.
```
  1 9 7
+ 1 0 3
-------
```

i.
```
  5 0 9
-   1 5
-------
```

j.
```
  3 3 7
  2 0 3
+   8 4
-------
```

k.
```
  2 0 0
- 1 0 0
-------
```

l.
```
  9 8 0
- 2 6 5
-------
```

m.
```
  3 2
    8
+ 6 4
-----
```

a. Find the sum and difference as directed.

b. Colour the shape according to the colours given below.

0 to 250	blue	251 to 500	yellow
501 to 750	green	751 to 999	red

3. Multiply

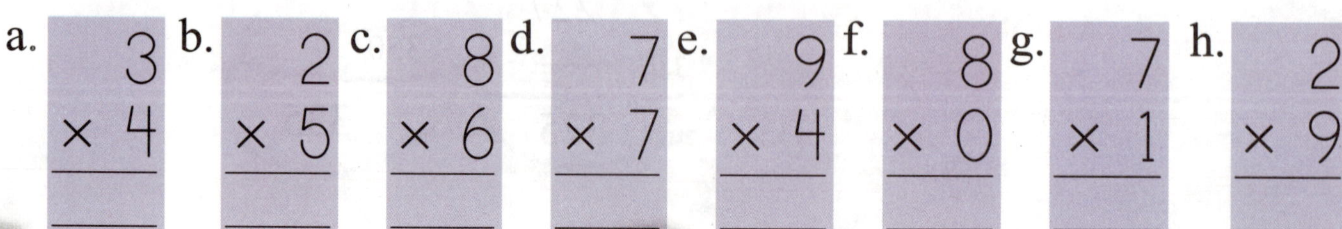

a. 3 × 4 b. 2 × 5 c. 8 × 6 d. 7 × 7 e. 9 × 4 f. 8 × 0 g. 7 × 1 h. 2 × 9

4. Fill in the boxes.

a. 6 tens less than 600 is __________

b. In 932 the digit 3 is in __________ place.

c. 100 more than 726 is __________.

d. 20 more than 693 is __________.

e. Nine hundred nine in numeral is __________.

f. 306 is __________ more than 276

g. Difference between 4×3 and 24÷4 is __________.

5. Multiplication is repeated addition. Now add and fill in these boxes.

a. 3 × 5 = 5 + 5 + 5 = 15

b. 6 × 3 = ☐ = ☐

c. 5 × 2 = ☐ = ☐

d. 4 × 8 = ☐ = ☐

e. 2 × 9 = ☐ = ☐

f.

6. Write '<' or '>' in the circle

a. 173 ◯ 371 b. 104 ◯ 401 c. 281 ◯ 282

d. 365 ◯ 465 e. 296 ◯ 269 f. 695 ◯ 596

g. 654 ◯ 354 h. 458 ◯ 254 i. 284 ◯ 245

7. Shop and tell

a.

You bought	$	¢
A bat for	30	00
A book for	+25	00
Total money spent		

b.

	$	¢
You took	85	00
You spent	– 36	00
Total money left		

c.

You bought	$	¢
a box of crayons	27	00
a pen	+30	00
Total money spent		

d.

	$	¢
Father gave	100	00
I spent	– 75	00
Total money left with me		

8. What time is it?

a. 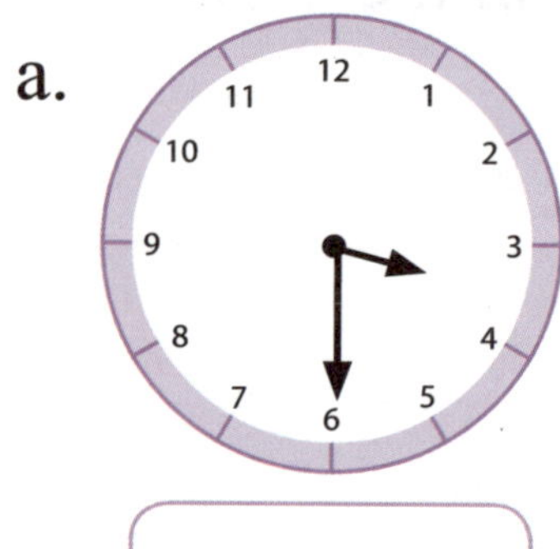

b. 

c. 

9. Show the time given on the clock.

a. 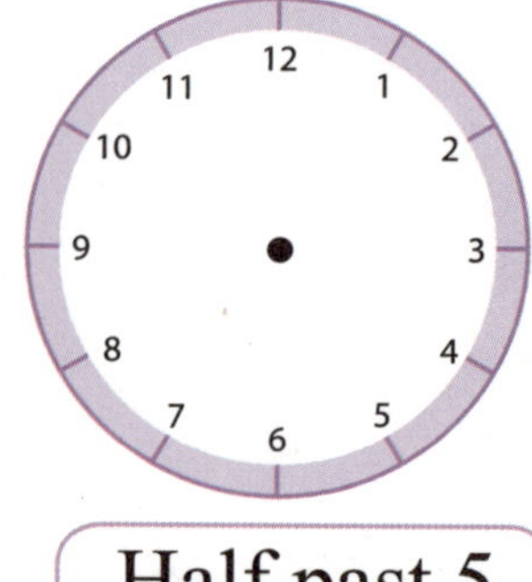

Half past 5

b. 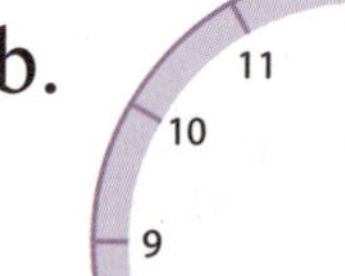

Half past 10

c. 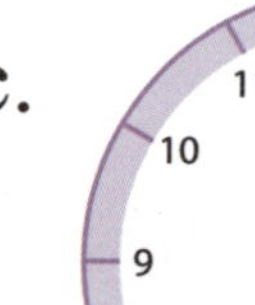

Half past 8

10. Write the names of the given shapes.

    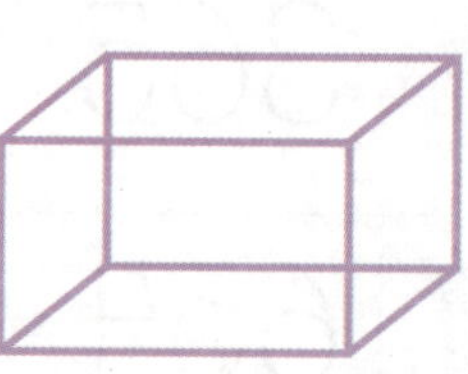

Word Problems

a. A cricketer was batting and was on 90. How many runs does he need to complete his century?

	90
+	
runs	100

b. Emma distributed 150 chocolates. 28 chocolates were still left with her. How many chocolates did Emma have in all?

	150
+	28
chocolates	

c. A train has 950 passengers. 341 passengers got down at Delhi. How many are left in the train?

	950
−	341
passengers	

d. Each room has eight bulbs. If in a building there are 7 rooms, find the total number of bulbs required.

	8
×	7
bulbs	

Numbers (Up to Ten Thousand)

2

We have ten fingers and there are ten digits. These 10 digits can make any number.

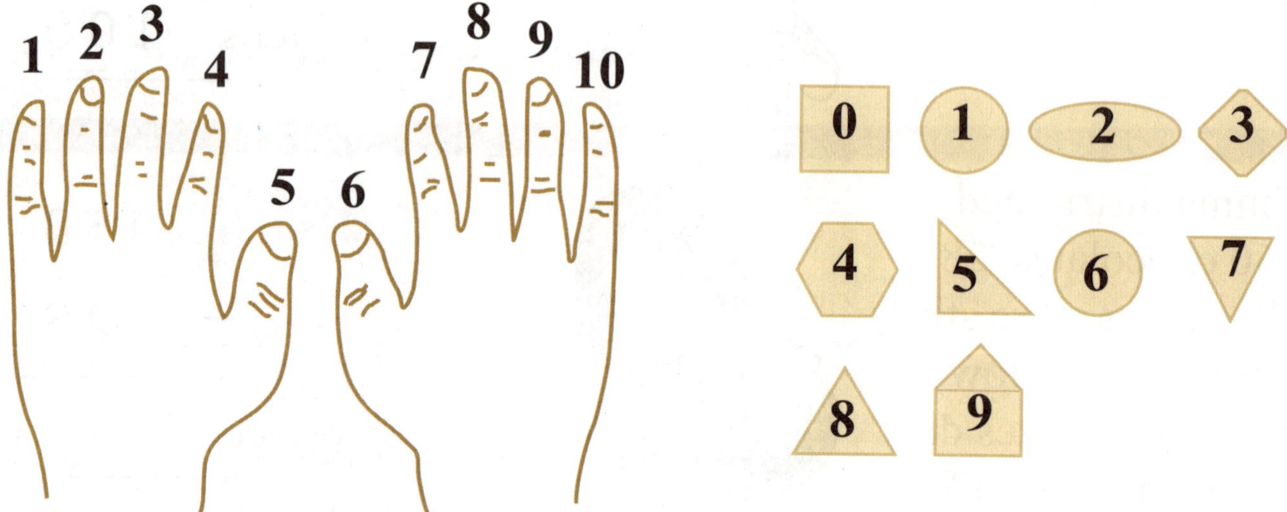

Take any one shape and it is a digit. You can take two shapes and get a 2-digit number like 43. You may also take 3 shapes and get a 3-digit number like 127.

{Largest single digit number) 9 + 1 = 10 (smallest 2-digit number}

{Largest 2-digit number) 99 + 1 = 100 (smallest three digit number}

{Largest 3-digit number) 999 + 1 = 1000 (smallest 4-digit number}

{Largest 4-digit number) 9999 + 1 = 10,000 (smallest 5-digit number}

Numbers 1,2,3.. are called counting numbers or natural numbers 0,1,2,3…….. are called whole numbers (0 with natural numbers are called whole numbers)

4-Digit Numbers

10 ones = 1 ten

10 tens = 100 = 1 hundred

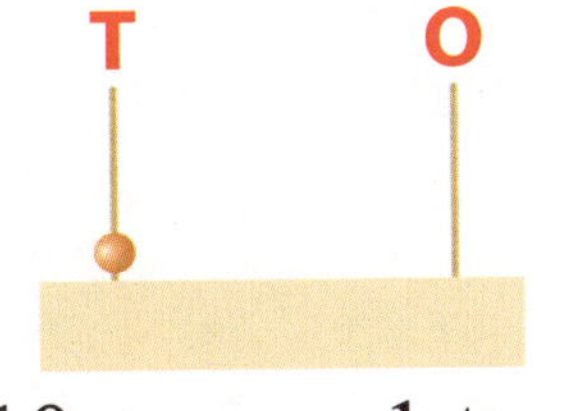

10 ones = 1 ten

10 tens = 1 hundred

H T O

9 9 9

What will be 1 more than 999?

How do we show it on an abacus?

(A stick of the abacus cannot have more than 9 beads. So the tenth bead is shifted to the next stick on the left handside where the place value is changed.)

How will we show 999 + 1 = 1000 on an abacus?

A new stick representing the 'Thousands' place is introduced.

1000

1001

Numbers beyond Thousand

1000 – One thousand

1001 – One thousand one

1002 – One thousand two

1010 – One thousand ten

1100 – One thousand one hundred

On Abacus

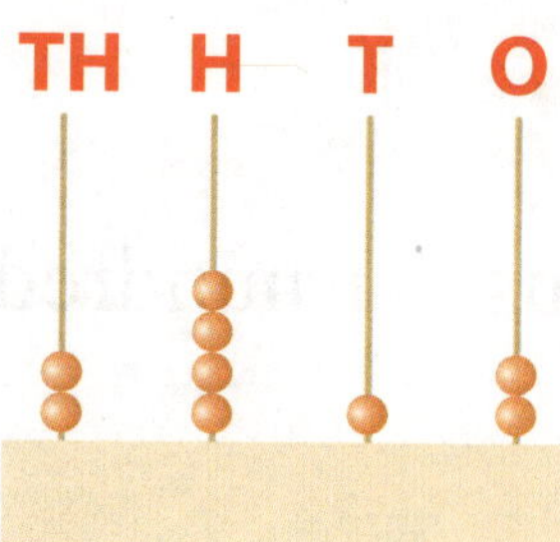

The number is 2412 (Two thousand four hundred twelve)

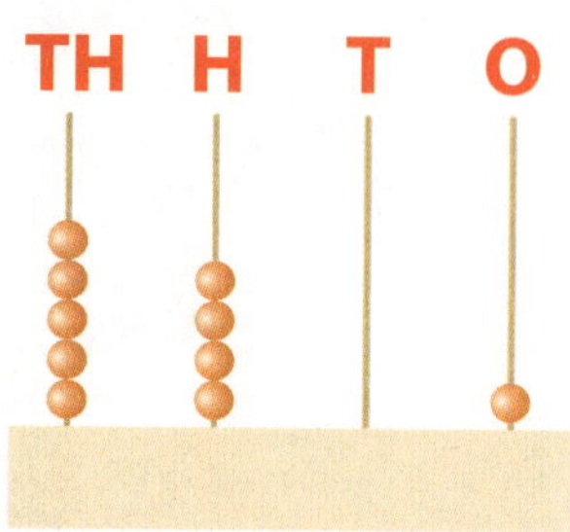

The number is 5401 (Five thousand four hundred one)

Exercise 2.1

1. Read the abacus and write the number and the number name.

a. 

____

b. 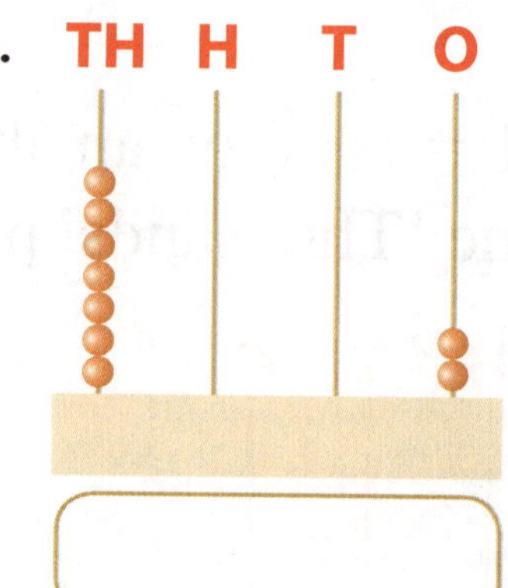

____

c. 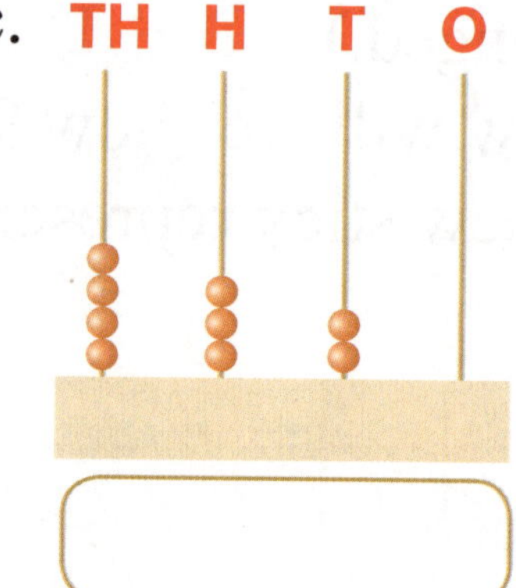

____

d. 

____

e. 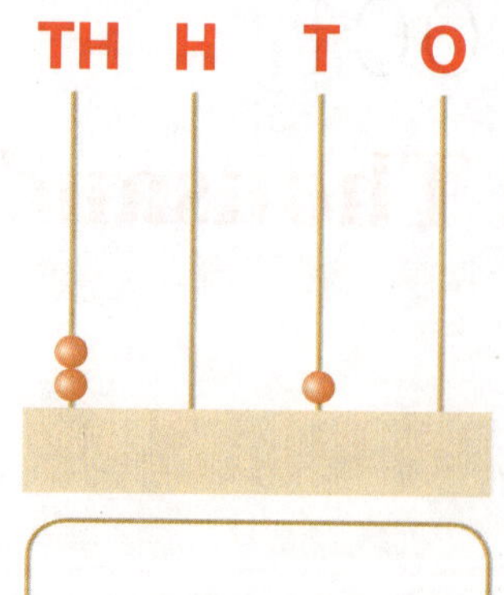

____

f. 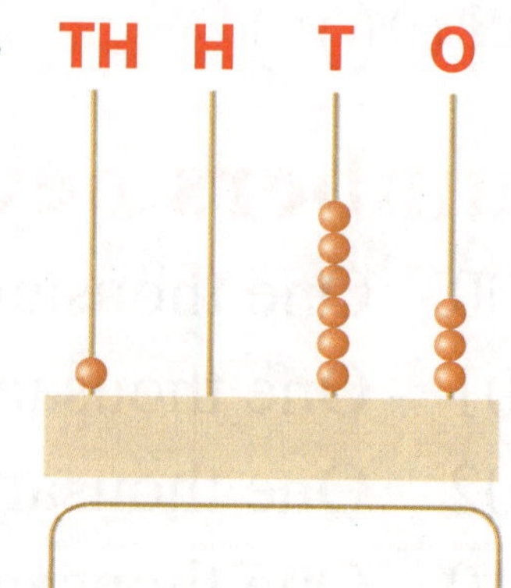

____

2. Show the number on the abacus and write the number name.

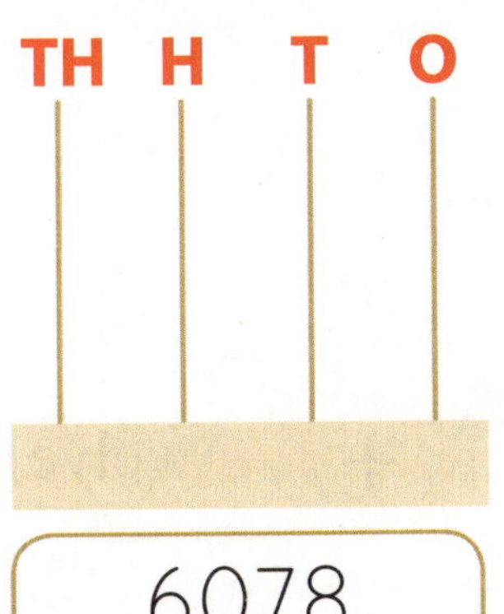

6078

9803

4520

_______________ _______________ _______________

3. Write the numbers for these number names.

a. Six thousand six hundred six ____________

b. Five thousand fifty ____________

c. One thousand twenty two ____________

d. Four thousand four ____________

e. Nine thousand five hundred seventy nine ____________

f. Eight thousand and eight ____________

g. Four thousand three hundred forty

Successor of a Number

Successor of a number is one more than the number

Successor of 3147 is 3148

Successor of 1620 is 1621

Successor of number = number + 1

Predecessor of a Number

Predecessor of a number is one less than the number

Predecessor of a number = number – 1

Predecessor of 254 = 254-1

= 253

Predecessor of 1960 = 1960-1

= 1959

Exercise 2.2

1. Write the following in expanded form.

a.	6854	=		+		+		+	
b.	3701	=		+	700	+		+	
c.	9190	=		+		+	90	+	
d.	2508	=		+		+		+	
e.	5273	=		+		+		+	
f.	4044	=		+		+		+	

2. Write in short form.

   a. Three thousand seven hundred __________
   b. One thousand sixty six __________
   c. Four thousand one hundred two __________
   d. Six thousand ten __________
   e. Nine thousand five __________
   f. Five thousand fifty __________
   g. Seven thousand seventy six __________
   h. Eight thousand eight hundred eight __________

3. Write the successor of the following numbers.

a. 1000 ☐	b. 4989 ☐	c. 3009 ☐
d. 2678 ☐	e. 5999 ☐	f. 2750 ☐

4. Write the predecessor of

a. ☐ 2680 b. ☐ 4001 c. ☐ 8000

d. ☐ 5210 e. ☐ 1000 f. ☐ 3100

5. Write the predecessor and successor of the given numbers.

	Predecessor	No.	Successor
a.		4090	
b.		3100	
c.		6154	
d.		5999	
e.		1390	
f.		2009	

Place Value

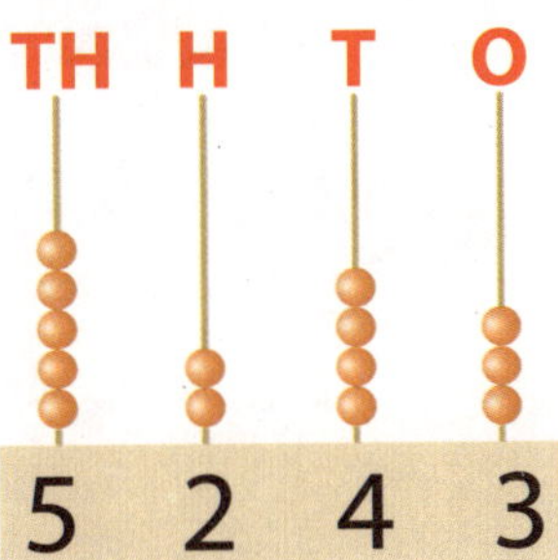

TH	H	T	O
5	2	4	3

Place value of 3 is 3 ones = 3

Place value of 4 is 4 tens = 40

Place value of 2 is 2 hundred = 200

Place value of 5 is 5 thousand = 5000

Place value of 0 is always 0

Place value of every digit is a number

EXAMPLE

Write the place value of the underlined digit <u>6</u>430 – Six thousand or 6000

Expanded form

Consider the number 8754.

Arrange it in a place value chart

TH	H	T	O
8	7	5	4

8754 = 8 thousands + 7 hundreds + 5 tens + 4 ones

= 8000 + 700 + 50 + 4

Expanded form

Expanded form of 3916

= 3000 + 900 + 10 + 6

TH	H	T	O
3	9	1	6

Write in short form

7000 + 700 + 50 + 3 = 7753

TH	H	T	O
7	7	5	3

Exercise 2.3

1. Write the short form

a. 9000 + 800 + 1 = ______

b. 3000 + 300 + 3 = ______

c. 5000 + 700 + 60 + 8 = ______

d. 1000 + 100 + 1 = ______

e. 2000 + 70 + 6 = ______

f. 8000 + 800 = ______

g. 6000 + 2 = ______

2. Write the place value of the underlined digits.

a. <u>6</u>851 =

b. 2<u>7</u>00 =

c. 34<u>0</u>9 =

d. 50<u>8</u>0 =

e. 144<u>1</u> =

f. 2<u>0</u>65 =

3. Counting by twos write numbers from:

a. 2374 to 2384

b. 6595 to 6605

c. 4006 to 4016

4. Counting by tens write numbers from:

a. 2870 to 2920

b. 6357 to 6407

c. 4492 to 4542

5. Counting by hundreds write numbers from:

a. 5690 to 6190

b. 2888 to 3388

c. 6601 to 7101

6. Understand the pattern and complete the rows.

a. 7095, 7097, 7099 ___ ___ ___ ___ ___

b. 3676, 3686, 3696 ___ ___ ___ ___ ___

c. 5505, 5605, 5705 ___ ___ ___ ___ ___

d. 2333, 2332, 2331 ___ ___ ___ ___ ___

7. Answer the following.

a. Give the number name of the number on the number plate of your father's car.

____

b. Write the number name of the year you were born in.

____

c. Write the number and the number name of the current year.

____

d. Write the number and number name of the year after 10 years (from this current year)

____

e. Write the number name for the year of independence.

____

f. Write the number name for the year of birth of Nelson Mandela.

____

Comparing Numbers

To compare numbers, we start by considering number of digits and then by writing place value of the digits.

EXAMPLE

Compare 4652 and 897

TH	H	T	O
4	6	5	2
	8	9	7

4652 has 4-digits and 897 has 3 digits
Hence, 4652 > 897

EXAMPLE

Compare 3625 and 5791

TH	H	T	O
3	6	2	5
5	7	9	1

Both have 4-digits. Take digits in the thousands place and compare
5 Thousands > 3 Thousands
So 3652 < 5791

EXAMPLE

Compare 6802 and 6384

Digits in thousands place are same, so we go to the hundreds place.
800 > 300
So, 6802 > 6384

TH	H	T	O
6	8	0	2
6	3	8	4

EXAMPLE

Compare 6453 and 6458

Since first 3 digits are same, we compare digits in the ones place.

TH	H	T	O
6	4	5	3
6	4	5	8

6453 < 6458

Since 3 < 8

So, 6453 < 6458

Ordering Numbers

Numbers can be arranged from smallest to greatest. It is called ascending order / increasing order.

Numbers can be arranged from greatest to smallest which is called the descending order / decreasing order.

Exercise 2.4

1. Compare the numbers and put the sign >, < or = in the space provided.

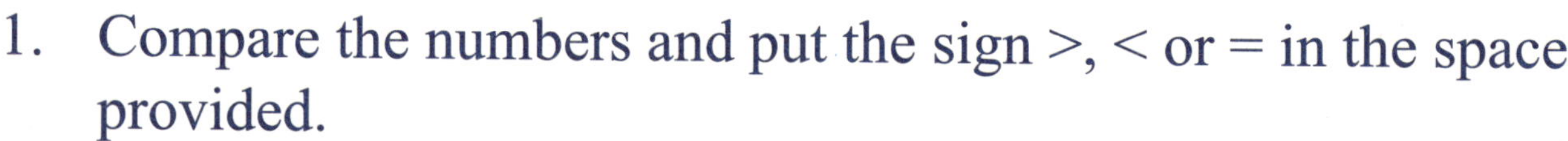

a. 4080 ◯ 8040 b. 2180 ◯ 2810 c. 6970 ◯ 9760

d. 6633 ◯ 6363 e. 4000 ◯ 3899 f. 7256 ◯ 7000

2. Arrange the following group of numbers in descending order.

a. 3721, 3725, 3729, 3724 ☐ ☐ ☐ ☐

b. 4608, 4680, 4689, 4674 ☐ ☐ ☐ ☐

c. 2105, 5012, 5102, 2015 ☐ ☐ ☐ ☐

3. Arrange the following group of numbers in ascending order.

a. 1234, 4321, 4231, 4132

b. 5067, 6057, 4067, 4076

c. 8010, 810, 81, 1080

4. Write four 3-digit and 4-digit numbers using 4, 0, 8, 6

a. 3-digit numbers

b. 4-digit numbers

5. Using the following digits make the largest and smallest number from each group. (one has been done for you)

	Digits	Largest	Smallest
a.	6,1,2,4	6 4 2 1	1 2 4 6
b.	3,9,0,7		
c.	1,8,4,0		
d.	6,5,0,5		
e.	1,2,3,4		
f.	1,4,7,6		

Mental Maths

Solve the crossword with the given clues.

1		2	3		4
		7			
		8			
				6	
5		10			
9					

Down

1. Successor of largest 3-digit number
2. 10 more than 4231
3. 8 hundred 3 ones
4. 200 less than 7100
5. is between 501 and 503
6. 6H + 6T + 6ones

Across

1. 1000+200+40+8
7. 2000 + 9
8. 4TH + 3H + 3T + 0 ones
9. Successor of 2139
10. Predecessor of 7362

Odd and Even Numbers

1, 2, 3, 4, 5…are counting numbers. When we start from 1 and skip counting by 2 we get 1, 3, 5… These are **odd numbers**. All numbers which have 1, 3, 5, 7, 9 in the ones place are odd numbers.

When we count 2, 4, 6, 8… They are **even numbers**.

Numbers which have 0, 2, 4, 6, 8 in their ones place are **even numbers**.

Interesting facts about odd and even numbers

1. 12 + 10 = 22

Even number + even number = even number

2. 13 + 4 = 17

Odd number + even number = odd number

3. 15 + 11 = 26

Odd number + odd number = even number

4. When an even number is divided by 2, remainder is always 0, [2 ÷ 2 = 1, R = 0]

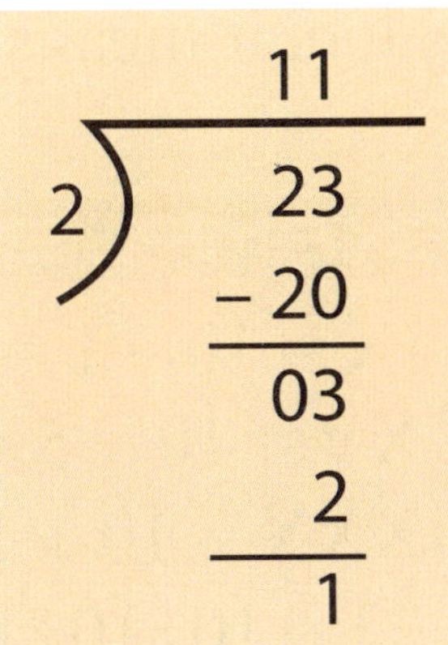

5. When an odd number is divided by 2, remainder is always 1. [15 ÷ 2, Q = 7, R = 1] 23 ÷ 2, Q = 11, R = 1

Roman Numbers

The numbers we know and use are called Indo-Arabic numerals. Eg. 0, 1, 2, ...

Hundreds of years ago, in the Roman empire the Romans used a different system of counting numbers.

The Romans used symbols for numbers.

Roman numeral	I	V	X	L	C	D	M
Indo-Arabic numeral	1	5	10	50	100	500	1000

In this class we will study - I, V and X

Reading Roman Numerals

I = 1 V = 5 X = 10

I	=	1	II	=	2
III	=	3	IV	=	4
V	=	5	VI	=	6
VII	=	7	VIII	=	8
IX	=	9	X	=	10

IV – If a Roman numeral of lesser value is written to the left of the bigger value, it means subtraction 5 – 1 = 4

VI – If a Roman numeral of lesser value is written to right of bigger value, it means addition. 5 + 1 = 6

EXAMPLE

IX = 10 – 1 = 9 XI = 10 + 1 = 11

XV = 10 + 5 = 15 XX = 10 + 10 = 20

XXX = 10 + 10 + 10 = 30 26 = 10 + 10 + 6 = X + X + VI = XXVI

33 = 10+10+10+3 = X+X+X+III = XXXIII

But is 40 = XXXX ? (we cannot use a symbol 4 times; so 40 is written as XL which we will study in the later classes)

XXIV = 10 + 10 + (5 – 1) = 24

Exercise 2.5

1. Fill in the numeral in front of each Roman number.

   a. I ☐

   b. III ☐

   c. V ☐

   d. VII ☐

   e. IX ☐

2. Fill in the Roman numeral for

   a. 11 ☐

   b. 12 ☐

   c. 13 ☐

   d. 14 ☐

   e. 17 ☐

   f. 18 ☐

   g. 19 ☐

   h. 20 ☐

3. Fill in the blanks with Roman numerals.

a. A football team has __________ players.

b. There are __________ months in a year.

c. After 5 years, you will be studying in class __________

d. 1 day = __________ hours.

e. Month of February has __________ days.

4. Write Roman numerals for:

a. 14 [ ]   b. 7 [ ]   c. 29 [ ]

d. 35 [ ]   e. 31 [ ]   f. 15 [ ]

5. Write Indo Arabic numerals for:

a. XXXIX [ ]   b. XVIII [ ]

c. XIII [ ]   d. XXXIV [ ]

e. XXVI [ ]   f. XIV [ ]

6. Put a (×) on the incorrect roman number and a tick on correct ones.

a. VIIII [ ]

b. XVV [ ]

c. XXVIII [ ]

d. XXXX [ ]

e. VVI [ ]

f. IX [ ]

Lab Activity

Aim: To represent a four digit number on abacus.

Materials required: A sheet of thermocol with 4 holes in a line, 4 sticks or pencils, beads or rings of 4 different colours.

Method:

1. Fix the four sticks or pencils in the holes.
2. Name the sticks from the right as ones, tens, hundreds, thousands
3. Use red beads or rings for ones place, blue for tens, yellow for hundreds and green for thousands.
4. Students should work in pairs and put their partners to callout the number and write the number on the abacus.
5. For eg. 3568 – Three thousand five hundred and sixty eight.
6. Can be repeated with different beads in each stick.

Conclusion: 4-digit numbers can be shown on the abacus.

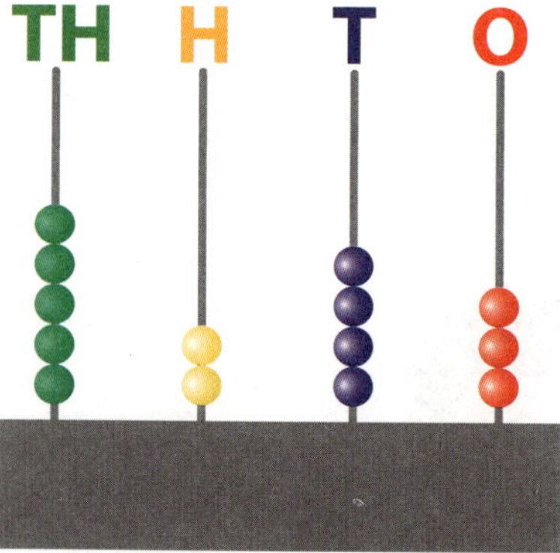

Addition of 4-Digit Numbers

3

TH	H	T	O
4	0	7	2
+3	8	6	9
7	9	4	1

Sum 7941

Step 1: Write the place value, then write the numbers one below the other.
Step 2: Add ones
Step 3: Add tens
Step 4: Add hundreds
Step 5: Add thousands
You get the sum.

Exercise 3.1

1. Arrange in columns then add the numbers and write the sum in words. One has been done for you.

TH	H	T	O
2	9	7	6
+3	7	5	2
6	7	2	8

a. 2976 and 3752
Six thousand seven hundred twenty eight.

b. 4684 and 7625 ________________

c. 8063, 1856 and 752 ________________

d. 1090, 901 and 91 ________________

e. 3744, 1432 and 869 ________________

f. 1748 and 2633 ________________

g. 2915, 529 and 59 ________________

h. 7, 6120 and 183 ________________

i. 2901, 543 and 36 ____________________

j. 3235 and 6198 ____________________

Some Special Properties of Addition

1. 17 + 21 = 38 and 21 + 17 = 38

   \ 17 + 21 = 21 + 17

   So, we see the sum of two numbers does not change when the order of numbers is changed.

2. (25+16) + 13 = 41 + 13 = 54

   25 + (16 + 13) = 25 + 29 = 54

   (25 + 13) + 16 = 38 + 16 = 54

   So, we see the sum of 3 or more numbers does not change even when their grouping is changed.

3. 493 + 0 = 493

   0 + 493 = 493

   This is a special property of '0'. Number + 0 = Number itself

4. 322 + 1 = 323

   Number + 1 = Its successor.

Addition with Regrouping

Regrouping of numbers

8 ones + 6 ones = 14 ones

Regroup 14 ones = 10 ones + 4 ones

= 1 ten + 4 ones

10 ones = 1 ten

EXAMPLE

Let us regroup and add.

(1) 4 tens + 17 ones

= 4 tens + 1 ten + 7 ones

= 5 tens + 7 ones

= 57

(2) 2 hundreds + 16 tens + 12 ones

Regroup 16 tens

16 tens = 10 tens + 6 tens

= 1 hundred 6 tens

10 tens = 1 hundred

Regroup 12 ones

12 ones = 10 ones + 2 ones

= 1 ten + 2 ones

\ 2 hundreds 16 tens 12 ones

= 2H + 1H + 6T + 1T + 2 ones

= 3H + 7T + 2 ones

= 372

10 hundreds = 1 thousand

Exercise 3.2

1. Regroup and write the number.

a. 3 tens 13 ones

b. 24 tens 15 ones

c. 12 tens 17 ones

d. 3 hundred 46 ones

e. 16 tens 18 ones

f. 9 hundred 18 tens 3 ones

g. 12 hundred 34 tens

h. 7 hundred 45 tens

Addition of numbers horizontally

Add by regrouping

1.
TO TO
3 7 + 4 6
= 7 T 13 ones
= 7 T + 1 T + 3 ones
= 8 T + 3 ones
= 83

2.
TO TO
7 9 + 2 5
= 9 T 14 ones
= 9 T + 1 T + 4 ones
= 10 T 4 ones
= 104

EXAMPLE

Write the missing numbers.

	3	6	
+		1	2
	8		5

Step 1 : ? + 2 = 5
∴ 3 + 2 = 5
Step 2 : 6 + 1 = 7
Step 3 : 3 + ? = 8
Step 4 : 3 + 5 = 8

So,

	3	6	3
+	5	1	2
	8	7	5

Exercise 3.3

1. Fill in the blanks.

a. 69 + 18 = ______ = ____

b. 56 + 27 = ______ = ____

c. 104 + 239 = ______ = ____

d. 321 + 76 = ______ = ____

2. Fill in the missing numbers.

a.

	7	2		5
+	1	4	3	
	8		7	6

d.

	2	5		1
+		7	6	
	6		9	0

b.

	1		7
+		5	
		2	2

e.

	1		7	4
+		8	9	
	5	8		1

c.

	5	4	3	2
+				
	8	7	7	3

f.

	3	5		2
+		7	4	
	6		5	7

Word Problems

In a train there are 2109 men, 3567 women and 3984 children? How many people are traveling in the train?

		① ① ②
Solution:	Number of men in train	= 2 1 0 9
	Number of women in train	= 3 5 6 7
	Number of children in train	= 3 9 8 4
	∴ Total number of people in train	= 9 6 6 0

Exercise 3.4

1. Solve the following word problems.

   a. For a concert of a rock band 2345 tickets were sold on the first day, 2872 on the second day and 3009 on the third day. How many tickets were sold in all for the concert?

   b. There were 3 bags with 5872 clips in the first bag 2109 clips in the second bag and 860 clips in the third bag. How many clips were there in all?

   c. There are 3500 books in the library of my school. The library in Roxanne's school has 1550 more books. How many books are there in Roxanne's school library?

   d. On Sunday, 4180 people visited the Pharaos. On Monday 3199 people and on Tuesday 2347. How many people visited the Pharaos on these 3 days?

   e. The distance between New York and London is 5567 km and distance between London and California is 8558 km. How much distance did Sam cover if he travelled from New York to London to California?

Lab Activity

Aim: To find sum of 3-digit numbers using the abacus

Materials required: A piece of thermocol with 3 holes at equal distance and in a line, beads or rings of 3 different colours

Method

Make an abacus with the 3 sticks (as described in Chapter 2 activity) and name them O,T,H

Add 235 and 412

First put 5 rings in ones, 3 in tens and 2 in hundreds. {use red for O, blue for T, and yellow for H}

For 412, put 2 more in 'O'

1 more in T

4 more in H

Conclusion: The ones stick has $5 + 2 = 7$ beads

The tens stick has $3 + 1 = 4$ beads

The hundreds stick has $2 + 4 = 6$ beads

Thus, $235 + 412 = 647$

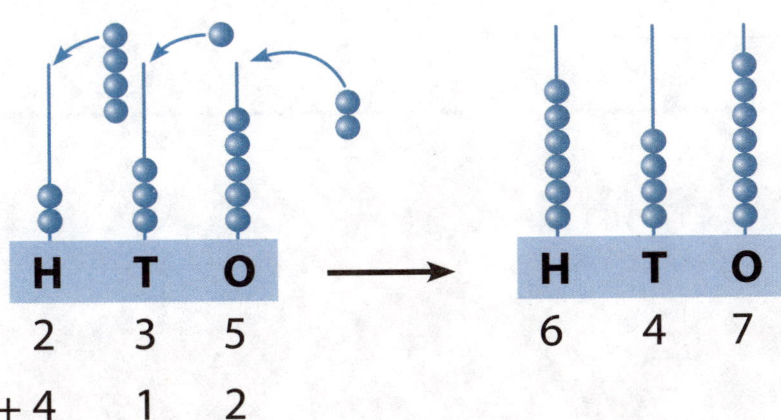

Mental Maths

1. Fillin the blanks

a. 7009 + ________ = 7010

b. 4209 + ________ = 4219

c. 3680 + ________ = 3700

d. 7055 + ________ = 9055

e. 2660 + ________ = 2960

f. 1090 + 0 = ________

g. 1364 + 2103 = 2103 + ________

h. 30 more than 1197 is ________

i. 2002 + ________ = 4002

j. 5470 + ________ = 6470

k. 3164 + 100 = ________

l. 1673 + 400 = ________

m. 287 + ________ + 324 = 525 + ________ + 324

n. 6003 + 10 = ________

o. 4440 + 70 = ________

Subtraction

4

South Africa is playing on 103 runs. They will win if they score 154 runs. How many more runs do they need to win?

	H	T	O
	1	5	4
−	1	0	3
	0	5	1

Step 1: Subtract ones 4 – 3 = 1 ones

Step 2: Subtract tens 5 – 0 = 5 tens

Step 3: Subtract hundreds

They will win if they score 51 runs more after scoring 103 runs.

EXAMPLE

Subtract 753 from 879

	H	T	O	
	8	7	9	(Larger number)
−	7	5	3	(Smaller number)
	1	2	6	This is called the difference

Remember

The larger number is written above the smaller number

Exercise 4.1

1. Find the difference.

	a.	b.	c.	d.
	H T O	H T O	H T O	H T O
	648	964	290	236
	−407	−730	−130	−121
	___	___	___	___

Checking the answers

Larger number | Difference
Smaller number | Smaller number
Difference | Larger number

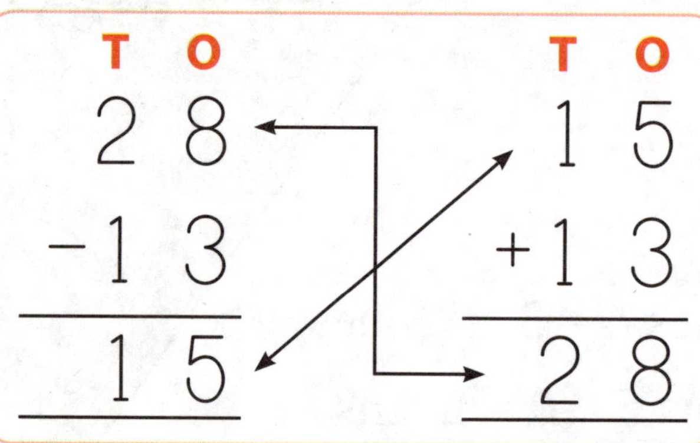

Larger number | Difference
Smaller number | Smaller number
Difference | Larger number

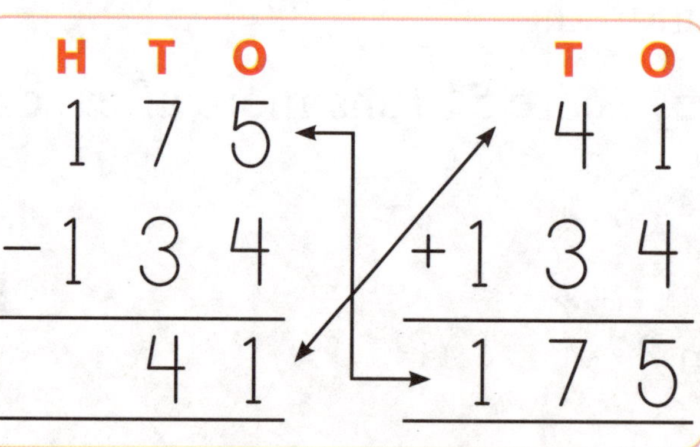

	H T O	H T O	
Larger number	888	111	Difference
Smaller number	−777	+777	Smaller number
Difference	111	888	Larger number

Subtraction of 4-digit numbers

EXAMPLE

Subtract 4704 from 7836

TH	H	T	O
7	8	3	6
−4	7	0	4
3	1	3	2

Step 1: Arrange numerals, then subtract ones
Step 2: Subtract tens
Step 3: Subtract hundreds
Step 4: Subtract thousands

Now, you get the difference.

Teacher should encourage students to add mentally and check the subtraction.

Exercise 4.2

1. Subtract the following

a.

TH	H	T	O
9	9	6	6
−7	7	4	4

b.

TH	H	T	O
5	0	5	0
−2	0	2	0

c.

TH	H	T	O
4	5	3	2
−3	5	3	1

d.

TH	H	T	O
9	4	8	7
−6	2	6	4

e.

TH	H	T	O
8	3	4	9
−7	1	2	9

f.

TH	H	T	O
7	6	6	6
−6	5	5	5

g.

TH	H	T	O
6	1	5	8
−5	0	4	8

h.

TH	H	T	O
2	4	4	4
	−3	0	3

Subtraction with borrowing

EXAMPLE

Subtract 4369 from 6532

TH	H	T	O
	4	12	12
6	~~5~~	~~3~~	~~2~~
−4	3	6	9
2	1	6	3

Step 1: Subtraction of ones 2 – 9 is not possible. Borrow 1 ten from 3 tens and it becomes 12 ones. 12 – 9 = 3 ones.

Step 2: 2 – 6 is possible. Borrow 1 hundred = 10 tens, 12 tens – 6 tens = 6 tens

Step 3: 4 H– 3 H = 1 H

Step 4: 6 Th – 4 Th = 2 Th

Checking the answer

```
   1 1
 2 1 6 3   ← Difference
+4 3 6 9   ← + Smaller number
 6 5 3 2     = Larger number
```

Hence, answer is correct.

Exercise 4.3

1. Subtract to find the difference.

a. TH H T O
```
 5121
-3265
```

b. TH H T O
```
 6702
-3429
```

c. TH H T O
```
 8800
-7777
```

d. TH H T O
```
 2861
- 399
```

e. TH H T O
```
 4541
-1978
```

f. TH H T O
```
 7040
-5935
```

g. TH H T O
```
 9642
-7647
```

h. TH H T O
```
 8003
-5498
```

2. Fill in the missing digits.

a.

b.

6	_	7	4
– _	2	8	_
6	5	9	0

c.

2	1	_	4
– 1	_	9	5
_	1	6	5

d.

7	_	4	_
– 4	3	8	7
2	8	7	1

Word Problems

Subtraction is very useful in real-life situations, especially when you pay for things you buy etc.

Example: Sam has \$ 100. After buying some stationery items, he is left with \$ 83. How much did he spend in the items?

Solution: Money with Sam = \$ 5000

Money left with him = – \$ 2232

∴ Money spent = \$ 2768

Money spent by Sam= \$ 2768

Example: Sum of 2 numbers is 2035. If one number is 1708, find the other number.

Solution: Sum of 2 numbers = \$ 2035

One of the numbers = – \$ 1708

1st number+2nd number = sum

1708 + ?	=	2035
Second number	=	2035 – 1708

$$\begin{array}{r} 2035 \\ -\,1708 \\ \hline 227 \\ \hline \end{array}$$

Second number is 227

Exercise 4.4

Solve the following word problems.

a. There are 2502 students in a school. Due to heavy rains 985 students were absent on a particular day. How many students were present on that day?

b. There were 6755 people watching a cricket match. After lunch only 3887 people were left in the stadium. How many left in the stadium?

c. Sid got 3420 points and Robby got 565 points less. How many points did Robby get?

d. A shopkeeper sold 5440 candles in the first week. Next week he sold 1648 candles less. How many candles did he sell in the next week?

e. 3500 people can sit in a hall. But 4125 people assembled to watch the play. How many people were extra than the hall's capacity?

f. In a bangle factory 8000 bangles are produced every day. On a particular day, due to some problem 1550 less bangles were made. How many bangles were produced on that day?

Exercise 4.5

1. Solve the following words problems.
   a. Subtract 2675 from the sum of 2838 and 4069.
   b. 2500 students went on excursion. 845 went to Cape Town, 927 to Durban and the rest to Pretoria; How many students went to Pretoria?
   c. 3450 people were travelling in a train. 1256 people got down in the first stop and 950 boarded the train? How many people now travelled in the train after the first stop?
   d. The Football club had 1200 members in the first year. In the second year 725 more members joined and 359 left. How many members were there at the end of the 2nd year?
   e. What number must be added to 6719 to get 9000?

2. Relate to these and find the solutions.
   a. The U.S. became independent in 1783. How many years have passed since then? ________________
   b. My Grandfather died 15 years later. In which year did he die?
      ____
   c. If Abraham Lincoln's 150th birth anniversary was celebrated in 2015, when was he born? ________________

Lab Activity

Aim: To subtract 3-digit numbers with abacus

Materials required: A thermocol piece with 3 holes at equal distance and in a line, beads or rings of 3 different colours

Method

Like in addition we make an abacus and use different coloured beads or rings for O, T, H.

Subtract 378 from 490

Show 490 on the abacus

Remove 378

Start from '0'. 0-8 not possible. Take one from 9 T and put 10 in '0'. Now 8 in T. Remove 8 from '0', 7 from T & 3 from 'H' what is left is the answer = 112

Mental Maths

1. Fill in the blanks (based on subtraction).

   a. 265 – ________ = 265

   b. 40 less than 95 = ________

   c. 36 + ________ = 90

   d. ________ – 0 = 901

   e. 72 is ________ more than 25

   f. 40 – ________ = 40

   g. 36 is 10 more than ________

   h. 500 is ________ less than 1000

   i. 40 minus 26 gives ________

   j. 25 minus 2 dozens is ________

   k. 60 less than a century is ________

Multiplication

Multiplication is repeated addition.

There are 4 petals in each flower. If there are 3 flowers then how many petals are there in all?

We can add 4 + 4 + 4 = 12

We can also say 3 times 4 = 12

$3 \times 4 = 12$

12 is the **product**

Total number of wheels = 2 + 2 + 2 + 2 = 8

4 times 2 = $4 \times 2 = 8$

8 is the **product**

Multiplication is done by skip counting also.

5, 10, 15, 20, 25, 30, 35, 40, 45, 50

5 + 5 = 10, 5 + 5 + 5 = 15, 5 + 5 + 5 + 5 = 20, 5 + 5 + 5 + 5 + 5 = 25

This is how multiplication tables were generated.

Exercise 5.1

1. Let's see how much you remember.

a. 7 + 7 = 2 × 7 = 14

b. 9 + 9 = ___ = ___

c. 8 + 8 + 8 = ___ = ___

d. 6 + 6 + 6 + 6 + 6 = ___ = ___

e. 10 + 10 + 10 + 10 = ___ = ___

f. 4 + 4 + 4 + 4 + 4 + 4 = ___ = ___

g. 3 + 3 + 3 + 3 + 3 + 3 + 3 = ___ = ___

h. 2 + 2 + 2 = ___ = ___

i. 5 + 5 + 5 + 5 + 5 = ___ = ___

j. 11 + 11 + 11 = ___ = ___

k. 7 + 7 + 7 + 7 + 7 = ___ = ___

l. 12 + 12 + 12 = ___ = ___

Multiplication tables 2 to 10

Table of 2

1	×	2	=	2
2	×	2	=	
3	×	2	=	
4	×	2	=	
5	×	2	=	
6	×	2	=	
7	×	2	=	
8	×	2	=	
9	×	2	=	
10	×	2	=	

Table of 3

1	×	3	=	3
2	×	3	=	
3	×	3	=	
4	×	3	=	
5	×	3	=	
6	×	3	=	
7	×	3	=	
8	×	3	=	
9	×	3	=	
10	×	3	=	

Table of 4

1	×	4	=	4
2	×	4	=	
3	×	4	=	
4	×	4	=	
5	×	4	=	
6	×	4	=	
7	×	4	=	
8	×	4	=	
9	×	4	=	
10	×	4	=	

Table of 5

1	×	5	=	5
2	×	5	=	
3	×	5	=	
4	×	5	=	
5	×	5	=	
6	×	5	=	
7	×	5	=	
8	×	5	=	
9	×	5	=	
10	×	5	=	

Table of 6

1	×	6	=	6
2	×	6	=	
3	×	6	=	
4	×	6	=	
5	×	6	=	

6	×	6	=	
7	×	6	=	
8	×	6	=	
9	×	6	=	
10	×	6	=	

Table of 7

1	×	7	=	7
2	×	7	=	
3	×	7	=	
4	×	7	=	
5	×	7	=	

6	×	7	=	
7	×	7	=	
8	×	7	=	
9	×	7	=	
10	×	7	=	

Table of 8

1	×	8	=	8
2	×	8	=	
3	×	8	=	
4	×	8	=	
5	×	8	=	
6	×	8	=	
7	×	8	=	
8	×	8	=	
9	×	8	=	
10	×	8	=	

Table of 9

1	×	9	=	9
2	×	9	=	
3	×	9	=	
4	×	9	=	
5	×	9	=	
6	×	9	=	
7	×	9	=	
8	×	9	=	
9	×	9	=	
10	×	9	=	

Table of 10

1	×	10	=	10
2	×	10	=	
3	×	10	=	
4	×	10	=	
5	×	10	=	
6	×	10	=	
7	×	10	=	
8	×	10	=	
9	×	10	=	
10	×	10	=	

Properties of multiplication

We see $2 \times 8 = 16$, $8 \times 2 = 16$ } The product is the same

$5 \times 7 = 35$, $7 \times 5 = 35$ } The product is the same

When two numbers are multiplied, in any order, the product remains the same.

These are also known as the Multiplication facts

Multiplication with 1

$7 \times 1 = 7$, $1 \times 7 = 7$, $6 \times 1 = 6$, $1 \times 6 = 6$

$10 \times 1 = 10$, $1 \times 10 = 10$, $15 \times 1 = 15$, $1 \times 15 = 15$

Product of any number and 1 is the number itself. Number × 1 = Number

Multiplication with 0

$6 \times 0 = 0$, $0 \times 10 = 0$, $0 \times 12 = 0$, $9 \times 0 = 0$

Product of any number and 0 is always 0 Number $\times$ 0 = 0

Product of 3 numbers

Multiply $2 \times 3 \times 4$

$2 \times 3 = 6$ and $6 \times 4 = 24$

$2 \times 3 \times 4 = 24$

Let us see the product of $4 \times 2 \times 3$

$4 \times 2 = 8 \times 3 = 24$

So, $3 \times 4 \times 2 = 24$

$4 \times 3 \times 2 = 24$

So, we see when 3 numbers are multiplied in any order, the product remains the same.

Exercise 5.2

1. Fill in the blanks.

a. $7 \times 11 = 11 \times$ ☐

b. $39 \times 0 =$ ☐

c. $25 \times 16 \times 38 =$ ☐ $\times 38 \times 25$

d. $5000 \times 1 =$ ☐

e. $87 \times 1 =$ ☐

f. $418 \times$ ☐ $= 617 \times$ ☐

g. $999 \times 1 =$ ☐

h. $347 \times 186 \times 0 =$ ☐

i. $121 \times 200 \times 1 = 200 \times 1 \times$ ☐

Multiplication of a 2-digit number by a single digit no.

EXAMPLE

Multiply 24 by 2

H	T	O
	2	4
	×	2
	4	8

Step 1: Multiply $2 \times 4 = 8$ ones

Step 2: Multiply 2×2 tens = 4 tens

← Product

Multiply with carrying over

EXAMPLE

Multiply 25 by 3

H	T	O
	[1] 2	5
	×	3
	7	5

Step 1: Multiply 5 ones × 3 = 15 ones = 1 ten 5 ones

Write 5 under the ones column and carry over 1 to tens column.

Step 2: Multiply 2 tens × 3 = 6 tens

Add 1 written above = 6+1= 7 tens

EXAMPLE

Multiply 47 by 4

H	T	O
1	[2] 4	7
	×	4
1	8	8

Step 1: 7 ones × 4 = 28 ones = 2 tens + 8 ones write 8 under ones column carry over 2 to tens column

Step 2: 4 tens × 4 = 16 tens = 1 h + 6t = 1h + 6t Write 6 + 2 under tens & carry over 1 to hundreds.

Bring down 1. Multiplication of 3-digit number by a single digit (Without carrying over)

EXAMPLE

Multiply 123 by 3

H	T	O
1	2	3
	×	3
3	6	9

Step 1: 3 × 3 ones = 9 ones

Step 2: 3 × 2 tens = 6 tens

Write 6 under tens column

Step 3: 3 × 1 hundred = 3 hundred

← Product 369

Exercise 5.3

1. Find the product.

a. $\begin{array}{r} 34 \\ \times\ 2 \\ \hline \\ \hline \end{array}$ b. $\begin{array}{r} 42 \\ \times\ 2 \\ \hline \\ \hline \end{array}$ c. $\begin{array}{r} 44 \\ \times\ 2 \\ \hline \\ \hline \end{array}$ d. $\begin{array}{r} 23 \\ \times\ 3 \\ \hline \\ \hline \end{array}$ e. $\begin{array}{r} 33 \\ \times\ 3 \\ \hline \\ \hline \end{array}$

f. $\begin{array}{r} 134 \\ \times\ 2 \\ \hline \\ \hline \end{array}$ g. $\begin{array}{r} 104 \\ \times\ 3 \\ \hline \\ \hline \end{array}$ h. $\begin{array}{r} 222 \\ \times\ 4 \\ \hline \\ \hline \end{array}$ i. $\begin{array}{r} 203 \\ \times\ 3 \\ \hline \\ \hline \end{array}$ f. $\begin{array}{r} 321 \\ \times\ 4 \\ \hline \\ \hline \end{array}$

k. $\begin{array}{r} 73 \\ \times\ 3 \\ \hline \\ \hline \end{array}$ l. $\begin{array}{r} 602 \\ \times\ 4 \\ \hline \\ \hline \end{array}$ m. $\begin{array}{r} 412 \\ \times\ 3 \\ \hline \\ \hline \end{array}$ n. $\begin{array}{r} 704 \\ \times\ 2 \\ \hline \\ \hline \end{array}$ o. $\begin{array}{r} 523 \\ \times\ 4 \\ \hline \\ \hline \end{array}$

2. Multiply

a. $\begin{array}{r} 76 \\ \times\ 3 \\ \hline \end{array}$ b. $\begin{array}{r} 48 \\ \times\ 4 \\ \hline \end{array}$ c. $\begin{array}{r} 76 \\ \times\ 4 \\ \hline \end{array}$ d. $\begin{array}{r} 85 \\ \times\ 2 \\ \hline \end{array}$ e. $\begin{array}{r} 29 \\ \times\ 7 \\ \hline \end{array}$

f. $\begin{array}{r} 90 \\ \times\ 8 \\ \hline \end{array}$ g. $\begin{array}{r} 56 \\ \times\ 3 \\ \hline \end{array}$ h. $\begin{array}{r} 34 \\ \times\ 9 \\ \hline \end{array}$ i. $\begin{array}{r} 35 \\ \times\ 5 \\ \hline \end{array}$ j. $\begin{array}{r} 77 \\ \times\ 6 \\ \hline \end{array}$

3. Multiply

a. $\begin{array}{r} 142 \\ \times\ 8 \\ \hline \end{array}$ b. $\begin{array}{r} 235 \\ \times\ 4 \\ \hline \end{array}$ c. $\begin{array}{r} 309 \\ \times\ 3 \\ \hline \end{array}$ d. $\begin{array}{r} 158 \\ \times\ 4 \\ \hline \end{array}$ e. $\begin{array}{r} 267 \\ \times\ 7 \\ \hline \end{array}$

f. $\begin{array}{r} 128 \\ \times\ 9 \\ \hline \end{array}$ g. $\begin{array}{r} 278 \\ \times\ 5 \\ \hline \end{array}$ h. $\begin{array}{r} 536 \\ \times\ 6 \\ \hline \end{array}$ i. $\begin{array}{r} 734 \\ \times\ 8 \\ \hline \end{array}$ j. $\begin{array}{r} 569 \\ \times\ 9 \\ \hline \end{array}$

Multiply by 10, 100, 1000 etc

$7 \times 10 = 70$

$38 \times 10 = 380$

(To multiply by 10, in the product 0 is written at the one place and the numerals shift forward towards the left)

So, $496 \times 10 = 4960$

$8 \times 100 = 800$

$21 \times 100 = 2100$

(To multiply by 100, add two zeros after the number, to its right)

Exercise 5.4

1. Find the product

a. $30 \times 10 = \square$

b. $269 \times 10 = \square$

c. $86 \times 100 = \square$

d. $10 \times 100 = \square$

e. $78 \times 100 = \square$

f. $873 \times 100 = \square$

2. Fill in the blanks.

a. $37 \times 100 =$ ________

b. ________ $\times 68 = 68$

c. $10 \times$ ________ $= 4900$

d. ________ $\times 21 = 2100$

e. ________ $\times 25 = 2500$

f. ________ $\times 194 = 0$

g. $87 \times$ ________ $= 8700$

h. $10 \times$ ________ $= 900$

Multiplication by 20, 30, 40, ... 90

EXAMPLE

$8 \times 20 = 8 \times 2$ tens = 16 tens = 160

$5 \times 30 = 5 \times 3$ tens = 15 tens = 150

When a number is multiplied by 10, 20, 30, 40, 50, 60, 70, 80, 90 then the number is multiplied by 1, 2, 3, 4, 5, 6, 7, 8, 9 and '0' is put to the right of the product.

Multiplication by 100, 200 900

$3 \times 100 = 3 \times 1$ hundred = 3 hundred = 300

$7 \times 200 = 7 \times 2$ hundred = 14 hundred = 1400

$13 \times 300 = 13 \times 3$ hundred = 39 hundred = 3900

When a number is multiplied by 100, 200, 300 .... 900, we multiply the given number by 1, 2, 3...9 and add two zeroes to the right of the product.

Exercise 5.5

1. Find the product

a.	34	×	20	=	
b.	17	×	30	=	
c.	24	×	400	=	
d.	13	×	500	=	
e.	161	×	40	=	
f.	48	×	100	=	
g.	84	×	20	=	
h.	3000	×	3	=	
i.	400	×	8	=	
j.	2	×	500	=	
k.	8	×	600	=	
l.	325	×	10	=	
m.	1	×	3000	=	
n.	10	×	500	=	

2. Solve the following word problems. (one is done for you)

a. The cost of a pencil is \$ 5. Find the cost of 8 such pencils.

Cost of 1 pencil = \$ 5
Cost of 8 such pencils = 5 × 8 = \$ 40
Ans. = \$ 40

b. There are 5 dozen hair pins in a packet and there were 5 such packets. How many pins were there in all?

c. There are 24 hours in a day. How many hours are there in 10 days?

d. Rick plays for 3 hours every day. How many hours does he play in 3 weeks?

e. A page has 25 lines. If there are 50 pages in a book, how many lines are there in the whole book?

f. A truck can carry 165 bags of cement. How many bags can the truck carry if it makes 20 trips?

A new property of multiplication

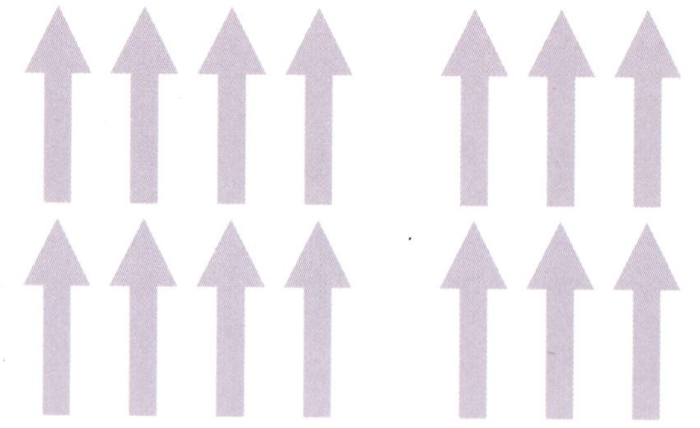

$\boxed{2} \times \boxed{7} = \boxed{14}$

$\boxed{2 \times 4} + \boxed{2 \times 3}$ Breaking up 7 into 4 & 3

$\boxed{8} + \boxed{6} = \boxed{14}$

$\boxed{3 \times 8} = \boxed{}$

$\boxed{3 \times 5} + \boxed{3 \times 3}$

$\boxed{} + \boxed{}$

$= \boxed{}$

So, $3 \times 8 = 3 \times 8\ (5 + 3)$

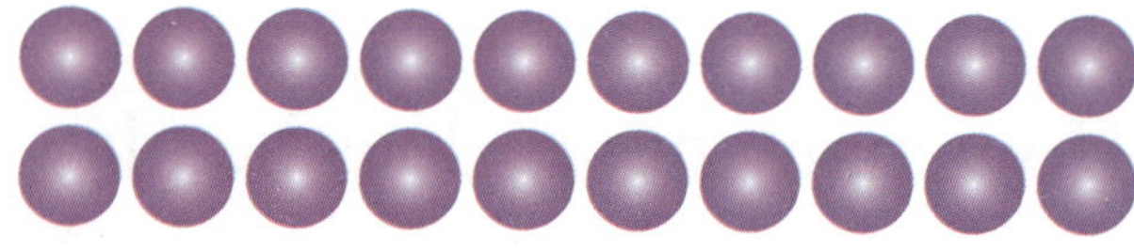

There are 2×10 beads = $\boxed{}$

If we split 10 as 8 + 2 we get thins

$2 \times 10 = 2 \times (\ 8 + 2\ )$

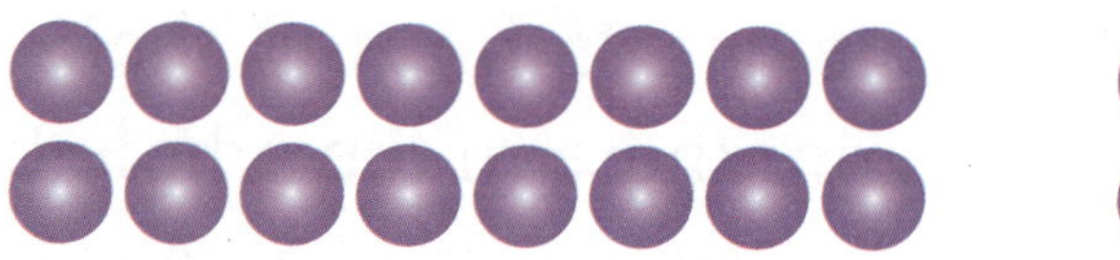

$2 \times 8 + 2 \times 2$

$16 + 4 = \square$

So, if we need to multiply

9×14

We can do $9 \times (10 + 4)$

$9 \times 10 + 9 \times 4$

$= 90 + 36$

OR we can say

$9 \times (10 + 4) = 9 \times 10 + 9 \times 4$

$= \square + \square$

$= \square$

Exercise 5.6

1. Write as shown.

a. $15 \times 13 = 15 \times (10 + 3) = 15 \times 10 + 15 \times 3 = 150 + 45 = 195$

b. $18 \times 17 = 18 \times (\square + \square) = \square + \square = \square + \square = \square$

c. $19 \times 23 = 19 \times (\square + \square) = \square + \square = \square + \square = \square$

d. $22 \times 11 = 22 \times (\square + \square) = \square + \square = \square + \square = \square$

EXAMPLE

Multiply 87×36

$87 \times 36 = 87 \times (30 + 6)$

$= 87 \times 30 + 87 \times 6$

$= 2610 + 522$

$= 3132$

There is another method.

TH	H	T	O
		8	7
	×	3	6
	5	2	2
2	6	1	0
3	1	3	2

Step 1: Multiply 87×6

Step 2: Multiply 87×30

∴ $87 \times 36 = 3132$

EXAMPLE

	H	T	O
		2	3
×		1	2
		4	6
	2	3	0
	2	7	6

Step 1: Multiply 23 × 2 = 46

Step 2: Multiply 23 × 10 = 230

EXAMPLE

Find the product of 45 and 28.

	H	T	O
	1	4	5
	×	2	8
1	1	6	0
2	9	0	0
4	0	6	0

Step 1: Multiply 145 × 8

Step 2: 145 × 20

Exercise 5.7

1. Find the product by forming sums

a.	38 × 23	f.	77 × 19	k.	84 × 28
b.	52 × 49	g.	93 × 35	l.	205 × 32
c.	304 × 14	h.	364 × 27	m.	169 × 36
d.	160 × 18	i.	289 × 26	n.	346 × 25
e.	176 × 24	j.	507 × 19	o.	188 × 36

Word Problems

Many real life situations involve multiplication.

Example: The price of a kettle is $ 50. How much would it cost to buy 19 such kettles.

Solution: Cost of 1 kettle = $ 50

Cost of 19 kettles = $ 50 × 19

Money spent = $ 950

```
     50
   × 19
    450
    500
  $ 950
```

Example: There are 12 eggs in 1 row of a carton. How many eggs are there in the carton, if there are 18 such rows?

Solution: Number of eggs in row = 12

Number of eggs in 18 rows = 12 × 18

There are 216 eggs in the carton.

```
    1 2
  × 1 8
    9 6
  1 2 0
  2 1 6
```

Exercise 5.8

1. Solve the following word problems.

   a. 165 toys can be packed in 1 box. How many toys can be packed in 35 such boxes?

   b. A block in our colony has 203 flats. How many flats are there in 18 such blocks?

   c. A box has 24 crayons. How many crayons are there in 317 such boxes?

   d. There are 85 sentences in one page. How many sentences are there in 110 such pages?

   e. 34 trees are planted in a row. How many trees are planted if 50 such rows are planted?

f. A box contains 58 books. How many books are there in 45 such boxes?

g. There are 22 coaches in a train. Each coach has 68 seats. What is the total number of seats in the train?

h. A factory produces 132 cycles every day. How many cycles does the factory produce in the month of March?

Mental Maths

1. Fill in the blanks

a. $126 \times$ _______ $\times 6 = 0$

b. $38 \times$ _______ $= 38$

c. $72 \times 41 = 41 \times$ _______

d. $9 + 9 + 9 + 9 =$ _______ $\times$ _______

e. 5 tricycles will have _______ wheels in all.

f. $320 \times 10 =$ _______

g. $5 \times$ _______ $= 250$

h. $10 \times 100 =$ _______

i. $7 \times 70 =$ _______

j. $8 \times 3 =$ _______

k. $10 \times 10 =$ _______

l. There are 12 books and each book has 10 pages. _______ pages in all

m. 1 pen costs \$10, 1 pencil \$ 5, So 5 pens and 10 pencils cost _______ altogether.

Division

6

Division is repeated subtraction

There are 15 notes. Divide them equally into equal groups of 5.

Take away 5 and put in 1 purse. 15 – 5 = 10

10 ones left

Take away 5 and put in 2nd purse. 10 – 5 = 5

5 are remaining.

Take away 5 and put in 3rd purse. 5 – 5 = 0

'0' notes are left.

15 ÷ 5 = 3 quotient.

On Number Line

Subtraction on a number line is done by jumping backward.

Division is repeated subtraction.

When we divide on a number line, we make equal jumps backward.

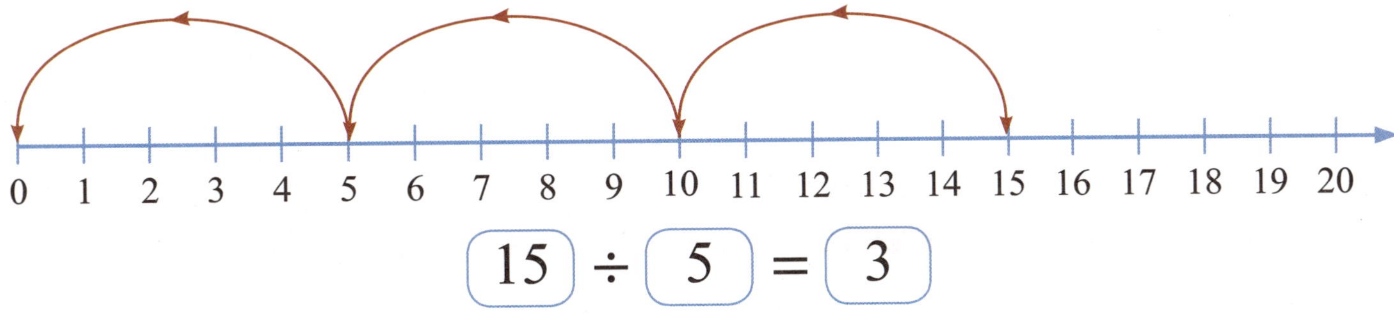

Is there any other way of reaching the start?

Can we reach the start from 15 taking equal backward jumps of 3? Let's see

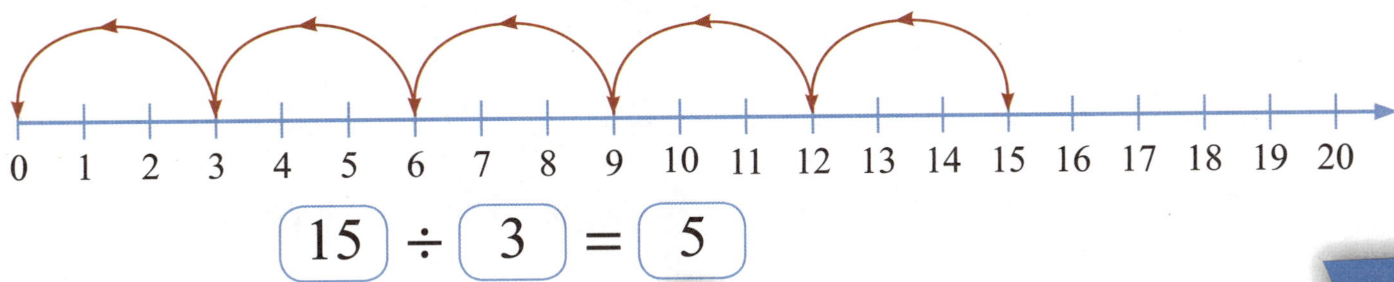

To reach the start by taking equal jumps backward, there are two ways.

$15 \div 5 = 3$

$15 \div 3 = 5$

$5 \times 3 = 15$ then $15 \div 5 = 3$ and $15 \div 3 = 5$

So, $3 \times 2 = 6$ then $6 \div 3 = 2$ and $6 \div 2 = 3$

$4 \times 3 = 12$ then $12 \div 3 =$ [4] and $12 \div 4 =$ [3]

These are called **Division facts**

Multiplication and division are inverse operations. For every multiplication fact there are two division facts

Exercise 6.1

1. Complete the following.

a. If [3] × [6] = [18] then [18] ÷ [3] = [ ] and [18] ÷ [6] = [ ]

b. If [2] × [5] = [10] then [10] ÷ [5] = [ ] and [10] ÷ [2] = [ ]

c. If [4] × [7] = [28] then [28] ÷ [7] = [ ] and [28] ÷ [ ] = [7]

d. If [3] × [6] = [30] then [ ] ÷ [5] = [6] and [ ] ÷ [6] = [5]

(Teacher should stress upon learning tables and computing mentally)

2. Try doing these. (Take the hints if needed)

		Hint
a.	[15] ÷ [5] = [ ]	[5] × [3] = [15]
b.	[20] ÷ [2] = [ ]	[2] × [10] = [20]
c.	[16] ÷ [2] = [ ]	[8] × [2] = [16]

d.	12	÷	4	=		4	×	3	=	12
e.	20	÷	5	=		5	×	4	=	20
f.	8	÷	4	=		4	×	2	=	8
g.	18	÷	3	=		3	×	6	=	18
h.	9	÷	3	=		3	×	3	=	9
i.	14	÷		=	2	7	×	2	=	14
j.	27	÷	9	=		9	×	3	=	27
k.	35	÷	5	=		5	×	7	=	35
l.		÷	6	=	7	7	×	6	=	42
m.	24	÷		=	8	8	×	3	=	24

3. Division is simple if you know multiplication tables. Use your multiplication tables to fill the boxes.

a.	28 ÷ 4 =		f.	20 ÷		= 2	k.	25 ÷ 5 =								
b.	30 ÷ 10 =		g.	16 ÷		= 4	l.		÷ 6 = 5							
c.		÷ 3 = 6	h.	27 ÷		= 3	m.	36 ÷		= 6						
d.	63 ÷ 7 =		i.	36 ÷		= 4	n.	24 ÷ 3 =								
e.	54 ÷ 9 =		j.		÷ 10 = 5		o.	20 ÷ 20 =								

4. Write division facts for each of these

a. $2 \times 3 = 6$ then $\underline{6} \div \underline{2} = \underline{3}$ and $\underline{6} \div \underline{3} = \underline{2}$

b. $2 \times 6 = 12$ then $\underline{12} \div \underline{2} = \underline{6}$ and ___ ÷ ___ = ___

c. $2 \times 9 = 18$ then ___ ÷ ___ = ___ and ___ ÷ ___ = ___

d. $2 \times 10 = 20$ then ___ ÷ ___ = ___ and ___ ÷ ___ = ___

e. $8 \times 5 = 40$ then ___ ÷ ___ = ___ and ___ ÷ ___ = ___

f. $4 \times 9 = 36$ then $\underline{36} \div \underline{4}$ = ___ and ___ ÷ ___ = ___

g. $7 \times 5 = 35$ then ___ ÷ ___ = ___ and ___ ÷ ___ = ___

h. $9 \times 7 = 63$ then ___ ÷ ___ = ___ and ___ ÷ ___ = ___

i. $8 \times 9 = 72$ then ___ ÷ ___ = ___ and ___ ÷ ___ = ___

Properties of Division

Any number divided by 1 gives the number itself as quotient.

$15 \div 1 = 15$ $\qquad$ $4 \div 1 = 4$

Any number divided by itself gives 1 as the quotient.

$20 \div 20 = 1$ $\qquad$ $184 \div 184 = 1$

When 0 is divided by any number, the quotient is always 0.

$0 \div 9 = 0$ $\qquad$ $0 \div 100 = 0$

Division by zero is not possible

Long Division

Divide 20 by 4

```
              5  → Quotient
         ________
Divisor 4 )  20  → Dividend
           - 20
           ____
              0  → Remainder
```

Dividend ↓ $20 \div 4 = 5$ ← Quotient; ↑ Divisor

Step 1: 4 × 5 ones = 20

Step 2: Write 20 below the dividend

Step 3: Subtract 20 from dividend

Step 4: 0 remains. We say remainder is 0

Check: 4 × 5 = 20 (divisor × quotient = dividend)

Exercise 6.2

Find the quotient: (Teacher should encourage students to check)

a. 3) 18

b. 

c. 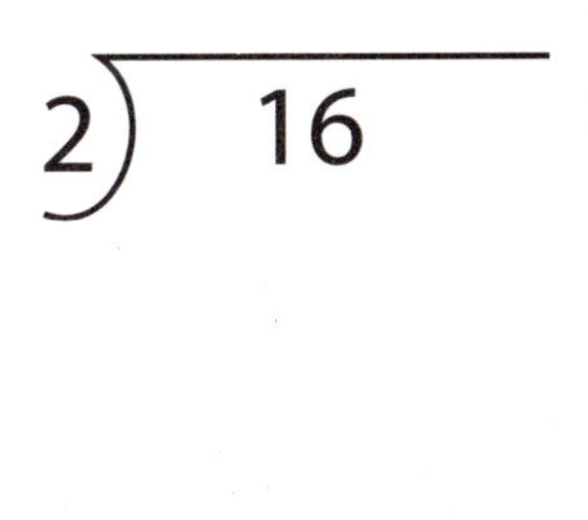

d. 5) 30

e. 

f. 7) 42

g. $8\overline{)\ 48}$

h. $9\overline{)\ 63}$

i. $6\overline{)\ 54}$

Division of 2-digit numbers

EXAMPLE

Divide 48 by 4

1 ten + 2 ones

$$\begin{array}{r} 4\overline{)\ 48} \\ -40 \\ \hline 8 \\ 8 \\ \hline 0 \end{array}$$

(4 × 1ten = 40)

(4 × 2 ones = 8)

T O

1 2 Quotient

$$\begin{array}{r} 4\overline{)\ 48} \\ -4\downarrow \\ \hline 08 \\ 8 \\ \hline 0 \end{array}$$

Remainder

1st method

(4 × 1 ten = 40)

48 ÷ 4

(4 × 2 ones = 8)

(4 tens 8 ones) ÷ 4

1 tens + 2 ones = 12

2nd method

Step1: Divide 4 tens by 4 and write 1 in tens column of quotient. Sub 4 – 4 = 0

Step2: Bring down 8 ones. 4 × 2 = 8, 8 ÷ 4 = 2 ones, write in ones column. Sub 8 – 8 and write 0 remainder.

Divide 69 by 3

```
   T O
   2 3
  ____
3) 6 9
 - 6↓
 ----
   0 9
     9
 ----
     0
```

Step1: 3 × 2 = 6 write 2 in tens place in quotient 6 – 6 = 0, bring down 9

Step2: 3 × 3 = 9, write 3 in ones columns in Quotient remainder 0

Exercise 6.3

1. Find the quotient

a. 48 ÷ 2 = ☐	e. 88 ÷ 4 = ☐	i. 93 ÷ 3 = ☐
b. 99 ÷ 9 = ☐	f. 77 ÷ 7 = ☐	j. 40 ÷ 4 = ☐
c. 86 ÷ 2 = ☐	g. 96 ÷ 3 = ☐	k. 69 ÷ 3 = ☐
d. 84 ÷ 4 = ☐	h. 68 ÷ 2 = ☐	l. 55 ÷ 5 = ☐

Division by re-grouping

Divide 36 by 2

```
   T O
   1 8
  ____
2) 3 6
 - 2↓
 ----
   1 6
 - 1 6
 ----
   0 0
```

Step1 : Divide 3 tens by 2
2 × 1 ten = 2 tens, write 1 in tens column in quotient. Write 2 below 3 tens
3 – 2 tens = 1 tens

Step2 : Bring down 6 ones 2 × 8 ones = 16 ones
Write 8 in ones columns in quotient.
Write 16 below 16
16 – 16 = 0 (remainder.)

Check : 2 × 18 = 36 (Divisor × Quotient = Dividend)

Division with Remainder

There are 4 children and 9 marbles. When divided equally, each child got 2 and 1 still remained.

ONES

$$\begin{array}{r|l} & 2 \\ \hline 4 & 9 \\ & -8 \\ \hline & 1 \end{array}$$

1 Remained $1 < 4$

Dividend = divisor × quotient + remainder

Divide:-

T O

$$\begin{array}{r|l} & 4 \\ \hline 6 & 27 \\ & -24 \\ \hline & 3 \end{array}$$

Q = 4
R = 3

$3 < 6$

Remainder < Divisor

Exercise 6.4

1. Divide, write quotient and remainder

a.	94 by 4	g.	68 by 7
b.	35 by 2	h.	74 by 3
c.	38 by 2	i.	34 by 4
d.	84 by 5	j.	79 by 6
e.	88 by 7	k.	99 by 8
f.	98 by 6	l.	79 by 5

Division of 3-digit numbers

1. Divide:- 244 ÷ 2

```
     H T O
     1 2 2
   ________
 2 ) 2 4 4
     2 ↓
   ______
     0 4
       4 ↓
   ______
       0 4
         4
   ______
         0
```

Q = 122
R = 0

2. Divide:- 303 ÷ 3

```
     H T O
     1 0 1
   ________
 3 ) 3 0 3
     3 ↓
   ______
     0 0
       0 ↓
   ______
       0 3
         3
   ______
         0
```

Q = 101
R = 0

Division with regrouping

1. Divide:- 756 by 6

```
     H T O
     1 2 6
   ________
 6 ) 7 5 6
   - 6 ↓
   ______
     1 5
   - 1 2 ↓
   ______
       3 6
     - 3 6
   ______
         0
```

Step 1: 6 × 1H = 6 Write 1 under hundred columns in quotient. Write 6 below 7. 7 – 6 = 1

Step 2: Bring down 5 tens 6 × 2 tens = 12 tens Write 2 under tens columns in Q. Write 12 below 15

Step 3: 15 – 12 tens = 3 tens. Bring down 6 ones. 6 × 6 = 36 Write 6 in ones columns in Q. 36 – 36 = 0

2. Divide: 460 by 5

```
  H T O
    9 2
   ------
5 ) 4 6 0
  - 4 5
  ------
      1 0
    - 1 0
  ------
        0
```

Step 1: 4 < 5. So, in such a case we take 46 tens
5 × 9 tens = 45 tens
9 is written under tens column in Q. Write 45 tens below 46.

Step 2: 46 – 45 tens = 1 ten. Bring down 0.
5 × 2 = 10
Write 2 under ones in Q.

Exercise 6.5

1. Divide, mention the quotient in the answer

a.	657 ÷ 3	d.	444 ÷ 6	g.	511 ÷ 7	j.	112 ÷ 8
b.	810 ÷ 9	e.	490 ÷ 5	h.	665 ÷ 7	k.	594 ÷ 6
c.	396 ÷ 4	f.	855 ÷ 5	i.	728 ÷ 8	l.	405 ÷ 9

Division by 10

1. Divide 85 by 10

```
     T O
       8   Quotient
    ------
10 ) 8 5
   - 8 0
   ------
       5   Remainder
```

2. Divide 764 by 10

```
     H T O
       7 6
    --------
10 ) 7 6 4
   - 7 0
   ------
       6 4
     - 6 0
     ------
         4   Remainder
```

(We see on dividing a number by 10 the number in the ones place is the remainder.)
{Division by 10 should be done mentally}

Exercise 6.6

1. Find Quotient and Remainder in the following questions.

a.	643 ÷ 2	h.	784 ÷ 3	o.	236 ÷ 6
b.	359 ÷ 4	i.	406 ÷ 8	p.	385 ÷ 6
c.	574 ÷ 7	j.	467 ÷ 9	q.	620 ÷ 4
d.	707 ÷ 5	k.	300 ÷ 3	r.	730 ÷ 8
e.	600 ÷ 9	l.	539 ÷ 4	s.	823 ÷ 9
f.	510 ÷ 2	m.	100 ÷ 6	t.	718 ÷ 9
g.	880 ÷ 4	n.	634 ÷ 7	u.	545 ÷ 5

2. Divide

a.	78 ÷ 10	d.	219 ÷ 10	g.	833 ÷ 10
b.	444 ÷ 10	e.	3438 ÷ 10	h.	7060 ÷ 10
c.	935 ÷ 10	f.	7777 ÷ 10	i.	107 ÷ 10

Word Problems

Example: If cost of a pen is $ 8, how many such pens can be bought for $ 504?

Solution: Total money = $ 504

Cost of 1 pen = $ 8

Number of pens that can be purchased = 63

So, 63 pens can be bought for $ 504

```
     63
8 ) 504
    48
    ---
     24
     24
    ---
      X
    ---
```

Example: The product of 2 numbers in 425. If one of them is 5, find the other number.

Solution: Product of two numbers = 425

One number = 5

So, the other number is = 425 ÷ 5

= 85

\ The other number is 85

$$\begin{array}{r} 85 \\ 5\overline{)425} \\ -40 \\ \hline 25 \\ 25 \\ \hline X \\ \hline \end{array}$$

Exercise 6.7

1. Solve the following word problems.

   a. 58 chocolates are distributed among 7 boys. How many chocolates does each boy get? How many chocolates are left?

   b. If 2008 oranges are packed in 8 baskets. Find the number of oranges in each basket, if all baskets have equal number of oranges.

   c. A factory produces 3760 bulbs in 5 days. If it produces same number of bulbs every day, how many does it produce in 1 day?

   d. There were 1840 books in a library? They had to be bound by 8 girls. If each girl was to get equal number of books. How many books did each girl bind?

   e. How many weeks are there in 3920 days?

   f. 9 students can sit on a bench. How many benches are needed to seat 540 students.

   g. A vendor sold 1694 toys in a week. How many toys did he sell in a day, if he sold equal number every day?

h. If the divisor is 9, quotient is 78 and remainder is 6, find the dividend.

i. A hare runs and covers 2 km in one hour. How much time does it take to cover 18 km?

j. An orchard has 408 trees. If there are 6 rows of trees with same number of trees in each row, how many trees are there in each row?

Lab Activity

Aim: To find division facts of a number

Materials required: 25 marbles

Method

1. Take 12 marbles and arrange them in a row
   $12 \div 12 = 1$ or $12 \div 1 = 12$
2. Arrange them in 2 rows with equal number in each row. It can be done in 2 rows and 6 columns.
   $12 \div 2 = 6$ or $12 \div 6 = 2$

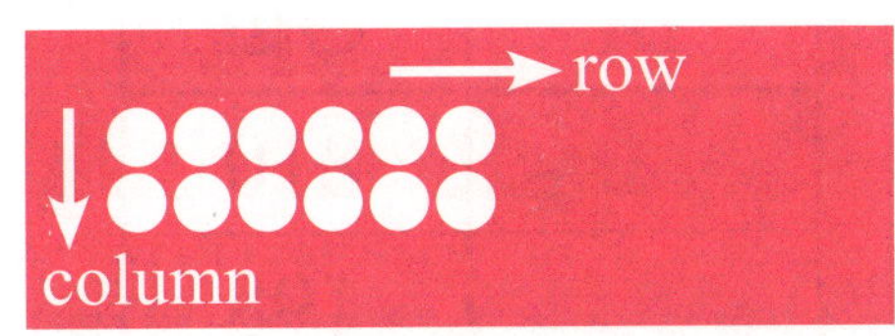

3. Show other combinations in same way
   $12 \div 3 = 4$ or $12 \div 4 = 3$

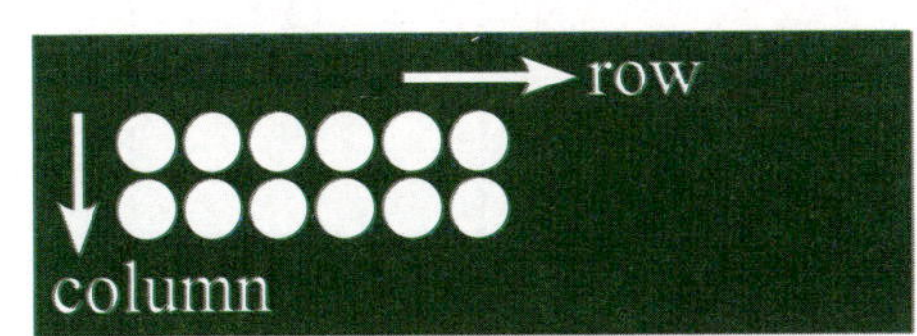

4. Do the same with 20, 24 marbles

Conclusion: The division facts of 12 are:

$12 \div 1 = 12$ $12 \div 12 = 1$
$12 \div 2 = 12$ $12 \div 6 = 2$
$12 \div 3 = 12$ $12 \div 4 = 3$

$20 \div 1 = 20$ $20 \div 20 = 1$
$20 \div 2 = 10$ $20 \div 10 = 2$
$20 \div 5 = 4$ $20 \div 4 = 5$

Mental Math

1. Mental Match, fill in the boxes

a. [ ] $\xrightarrow{+7}$ [35] $\xrightarrow{\div 5}$ [ ] $\xrightarrow{\times 7}$ [ ] $\xrightarrow{-7}$ [ ]

b. [ ] $\xrightarrow{+5}$ [ ] $\xrightarrow{\times 5}$ [50] $\xrightarrow{\div 5}$ [ ] $\xrightarrow{-5}$ [5]

c. [64] $\xrightarrow{\div 8}$ [ ] $\xrightarrow{\times 9}$ [ ] $\xrightarrow{+3}$ [ ] $\xrightarrow{-20}$ [ ]

d. [ ] $\xrightarrow{\times 10}$ [30] $\xrightarrow{\div 5}$ [ ] $\xrightarrow{+16}$ [ ] $\xrightarrow{-2}$ [ ]

This is a magical jug. All numbers that go in are multiplied by 9. These are the numbers that came out. What went in? Fill in the blanks as shown.

In	Out
	810
	198
	9
7	
10	

In	Out
	369
500	
	279
2	
	90

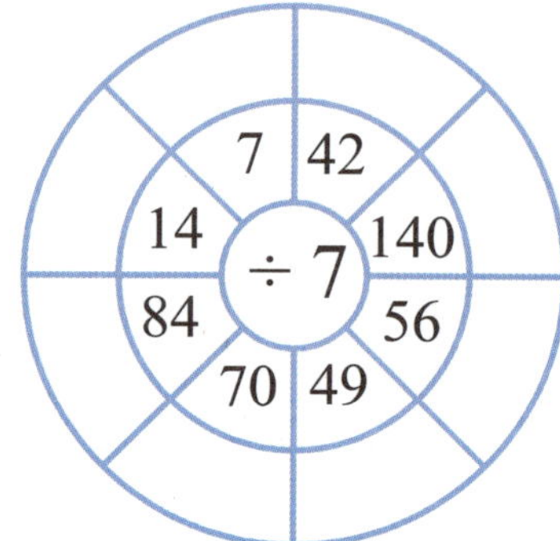

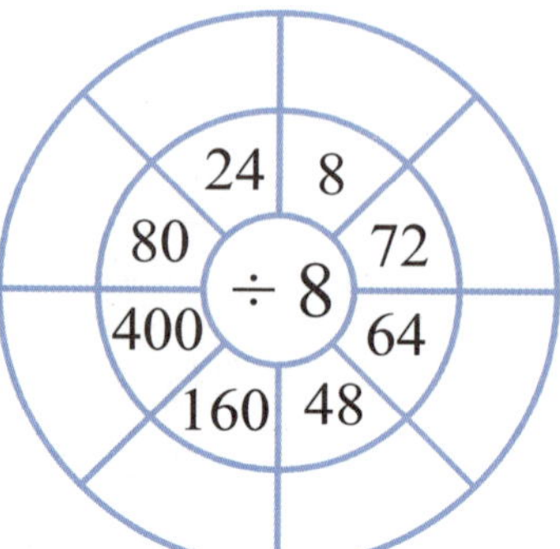

7 Fractions

Maria went home. She saw a bar of chocolate in the fridge. Her mother told her to share it with her brother Shaun. She divided it into two equal parts.

A fraction is a part of the whole

Each part is a fraction of the whole.

Half

When an object in divided into two equal parts, each part is called a half.

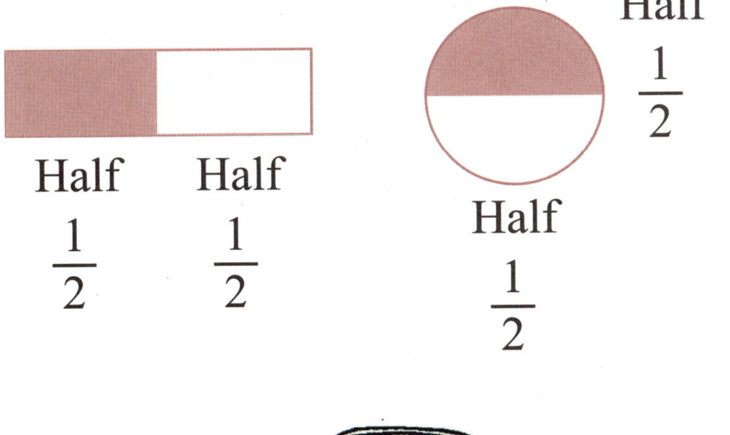

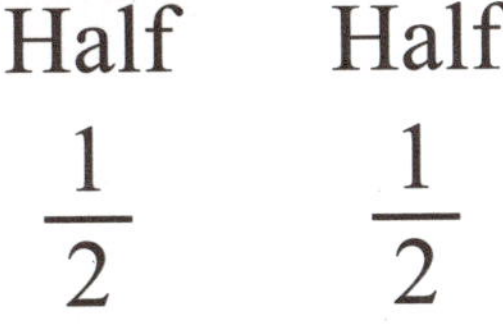

Exercise 7.1

1. Put a tick (✓) on the ones that show 2 equal parts.

a.

b.

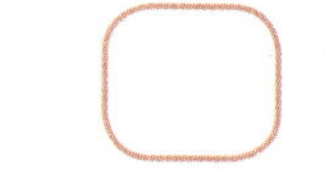

c.

d.

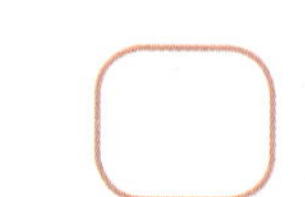

e.

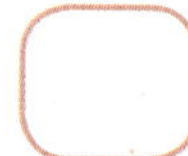

f.

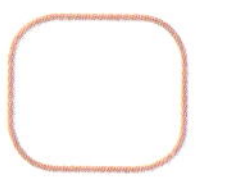

g.

h.

2. Find the shapes that show 2 equal parts. Colour half ($\frac{1}{2}$).

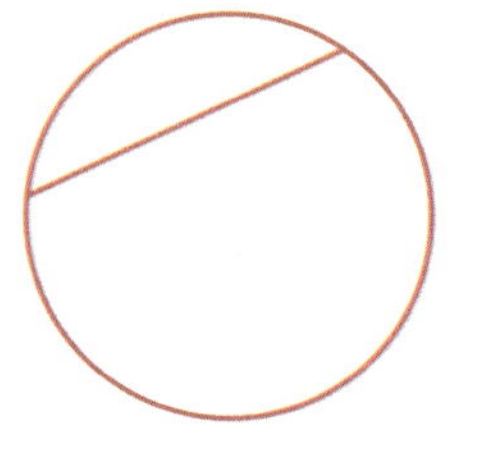
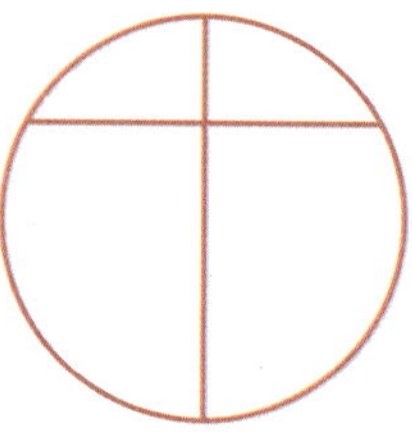
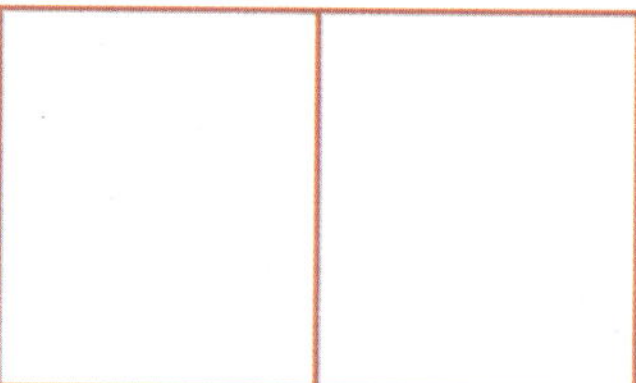
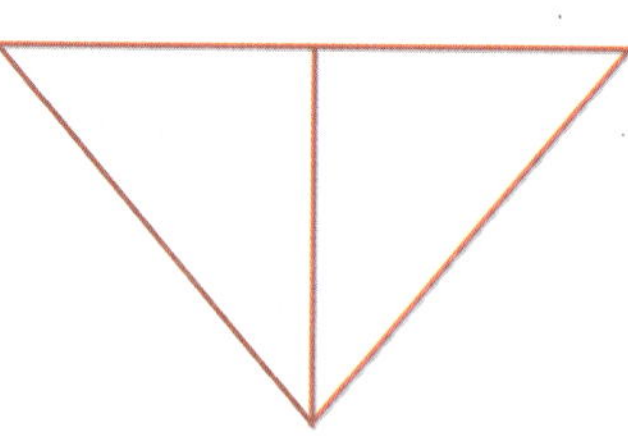

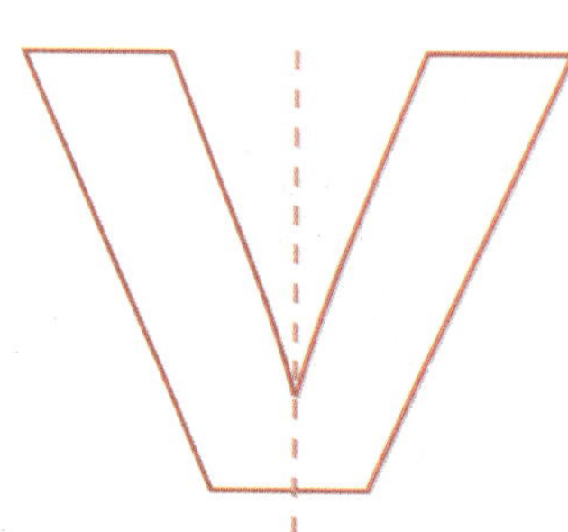
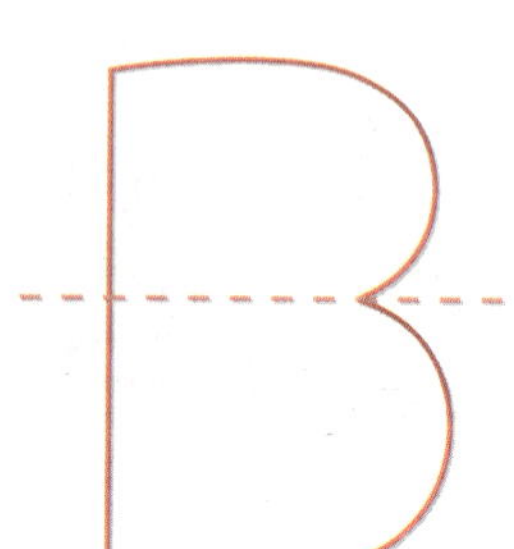

3. Colour half of the each group.

One third ($\frac{1}{3}$)

We can divide an object or a group into 3 equal parts. Each part is one third of the whole.

It is also written as $\frac{1}{3}$

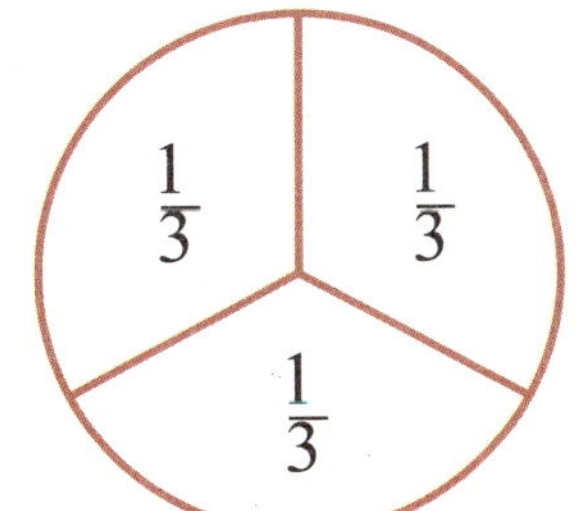

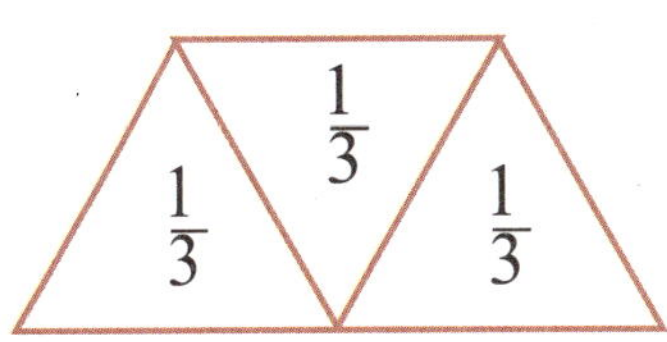

One fourth $\frac{1}{4}$

We can divide an object or a group into 4 equal parts. Each part is one fourth of the whole.

It is also written as $\frac{1}{4}$

$\frac{1}{2}$, $\frac{1}{3}$, $\frac{1}{4}$, are fractions.

This strip has been divided into 8 equal parts.

The shaded portion is $\frac{1}{8}$ numerator / denominator (one-eighths)

The denominator tells the total number of parts.

Exercise 7.2

1. Colour one thirds of each figure.

2. Colour one fourth of the following shapes.

3. Shade as instructed.

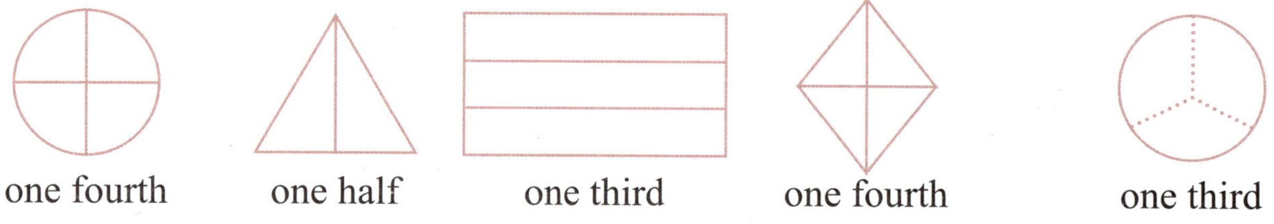

Numerator and Denominator

Maria got a big box of chocolates and divided into 10 equal parts. She gave Shaun 3 parts Shaun asked her, 'What is my share ?'

She told, ' $\frac{3}{10}$ (three-tenths)'

She told that 3 was the numerator and 10 was the denominator.

The denominator is the total number of parts and the numerator was his share.

She gave her father 1 piece and asked him his share.

Shaun told, '$\frac{1}{10}$ (one- tenth)'

Coloured portion is $\frac{2}{3}$ (two thirds)

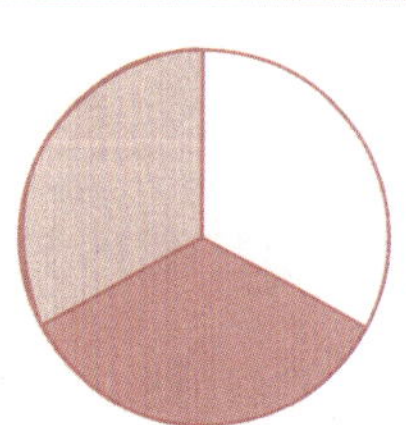

Exercise 7.3

1. Fill in the blanks.

	Fraction	Numerator	Denominator	Name
a.	$\frac{4}{7}$			four-sevenths
b.	$\frac{2}{3}$			
c.	$\frac{13}{20}$			
d.	$\frac{\square}{\square}$	3	8	three-eighths
e.	$\frac{8}{\square}$		11	eight-...............

2. Colour to show the fraction.

a. $\frac{5}{8}$ b. $\frac{1}{6}$ c. $\frac{3}{6}$

d. $\frac{7}{12}$ e. $\frac{4}{9}$

3. Write the fraction for the coloured / shaded part.

a. $\frac{\square}{\square}$ b. $\frac{\square}{\square}$ c. $\frac{\square}{\square}$

4. Tell what fraction of each coloumn does this figure have?

_______________ is black

_______________ is green

_______________ is red

_______________ is green and black

_______________ is coloured

_______________ is not coloured

5. Do you know fractions? Let's see.

a. What fractions of birds are flying?

b. What fraction of candles is burning?

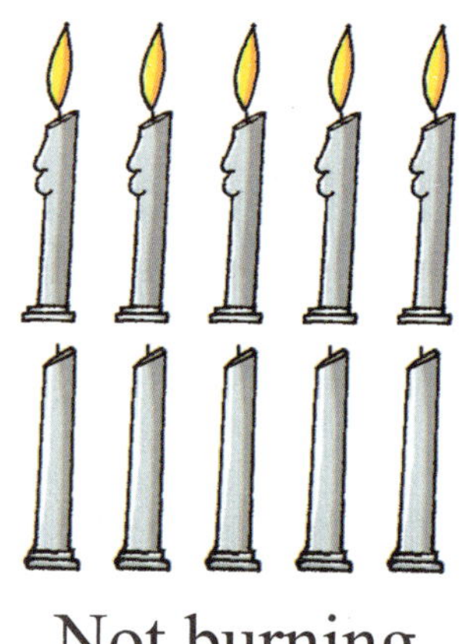

Not burning

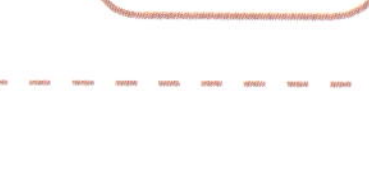

c. What fraction of children are girls?

d. What fraction of grapes are black?

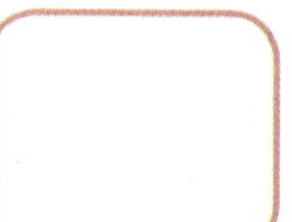

e. What fraction of the tiles are black?

f. What fraction is not shaded?

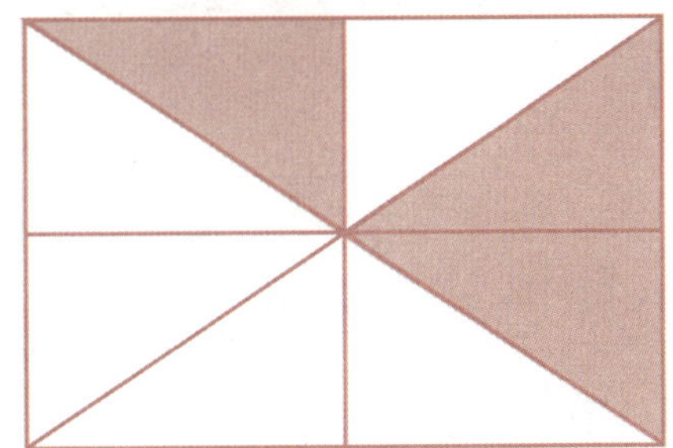

Lab Activity on Fractions

Children should be asked to bring paper strips, circles and triangles. Teacher should also bring objects like biscuits, a piece of bread, pizza base, a box of chalks, a box of pencils, paper strips, triangles, circles, should be pasted in the lab note books to show a whole.

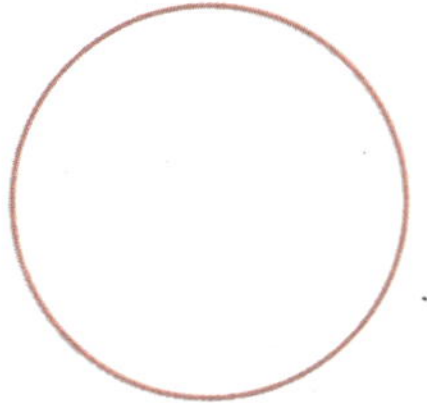

1 whole

1 whole

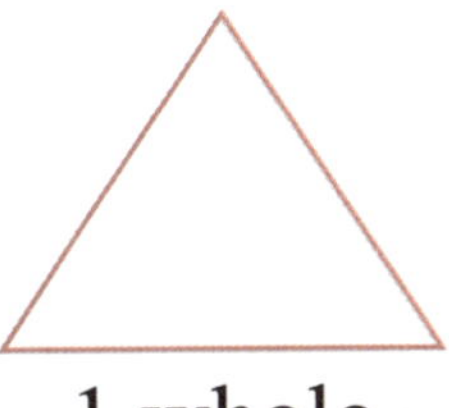

1 whole

The objects can also be shown to explain a whole.
Whole can be 1 object or a group of objects like a box of chalks, a box of pencils, a basket of fruits.

1 whole

Mental Math

1. In $\frac{2}{3}$, 2 is the __________ and __________ is 3.
2. The fraction three-sevenths is also written as __________
3. If we divide a pizza into 5 equal parts, each part is a __________. If my brother ate a few pieces of the pizza and only 1 piece is left, he ate __________ of the pizza.
4. Tick the shapes where $\frac{1}{2}$ is shaded.

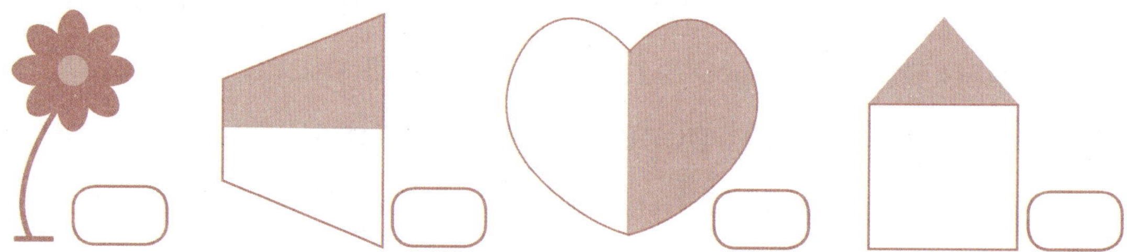

5. Tick the shapes where $\frac{2}{3}$ is shaded

6. Tick the shapes where $\frac{3}{4}$ is shaded

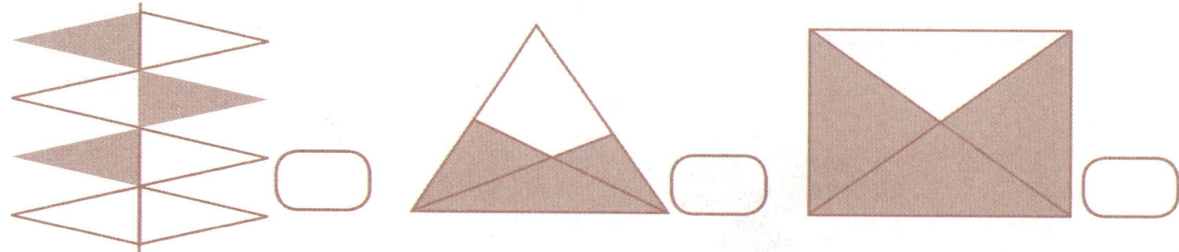

Time

8

Clocks or watches tell us the time. The face of a clock is called a dial.

It has 2 hands. The long hand is the **minute hand** and the short hand is the **hour hand**.

3 o' clock or 3:00

5 o' clock or 5:00

12 o' clock or 12:00

Exercise 8.1

1. Mention the correct time.

a.

b.

c.

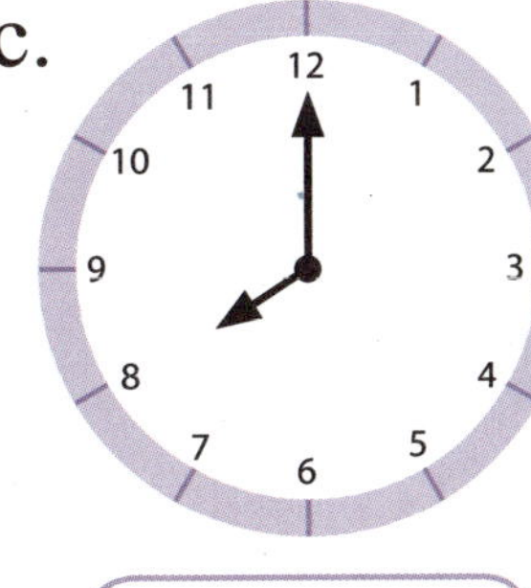

d.

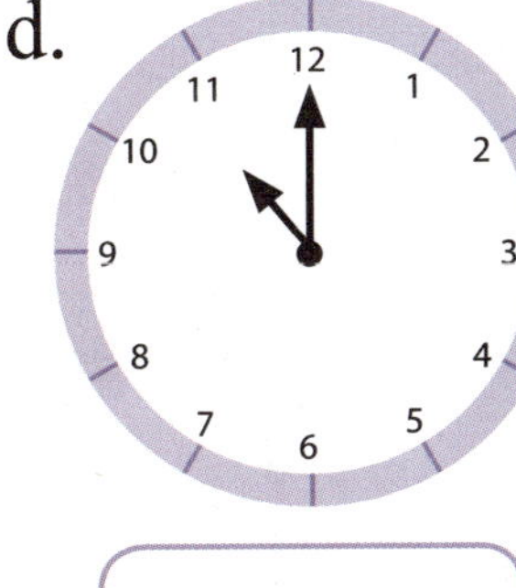

2. Draw the hands to show the time given below.

a.

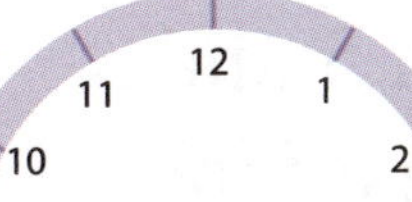

7 o' clock

b.

12 o' clock

c.

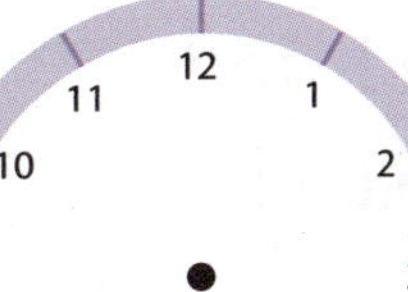

6 o' clock

d.

9 o' clock

Reading time in half hours

In 1 hour the minute hand completes one full round If it is at 12 at 4 o'clock, it reaches 12 again at 5 o'clock. When it moves half way round the clock it is at 6 and half past time.

half past 4 or 4:30

Reading time in half hours

Look at the position of the hands of the clocks.

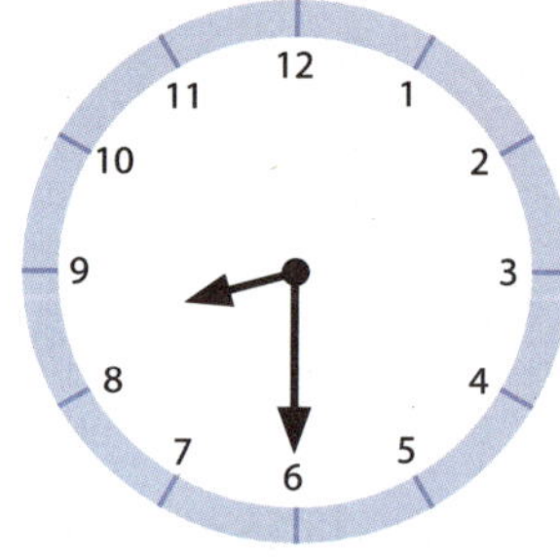

The minute hand is at 6. The hour hand is between 8 and 9. The time is half past 8 or 8:30

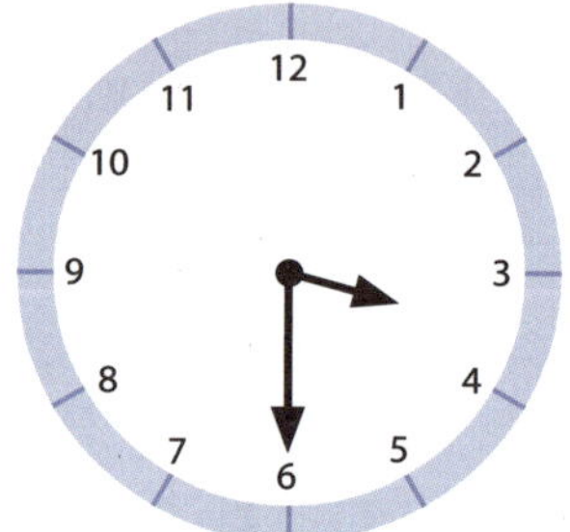

The minute hand is at 6. The hours hand is between 3 and 4. The time is half past 3 is 3:30

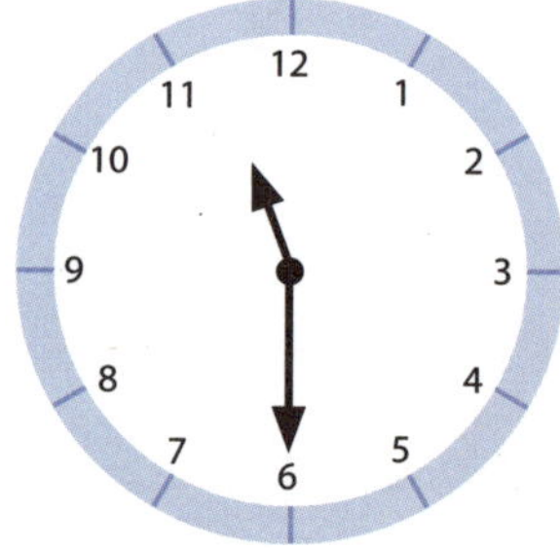

The minute hand is at 6. The hour hand is between 11 and 12. The time is half past 11 or 11:30

The minute hand is at 6. The hour hand is between 5 and 6. The time is half past 5 or 5:30

(When time is in half hours, the minute hand is at 6)

Exercise 8.2

1. Write the time under the clocks.

a. 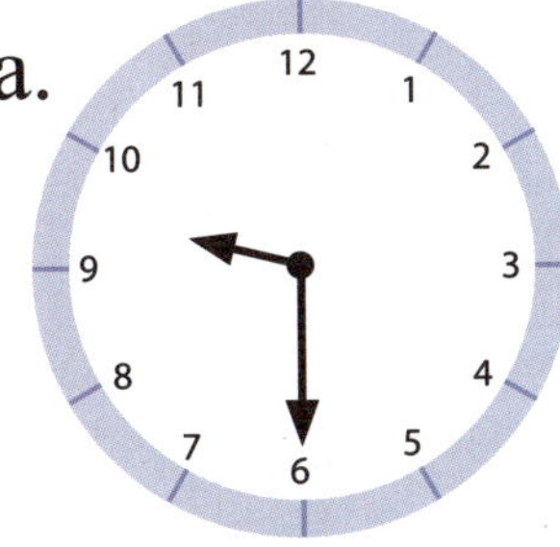

b. 

c. 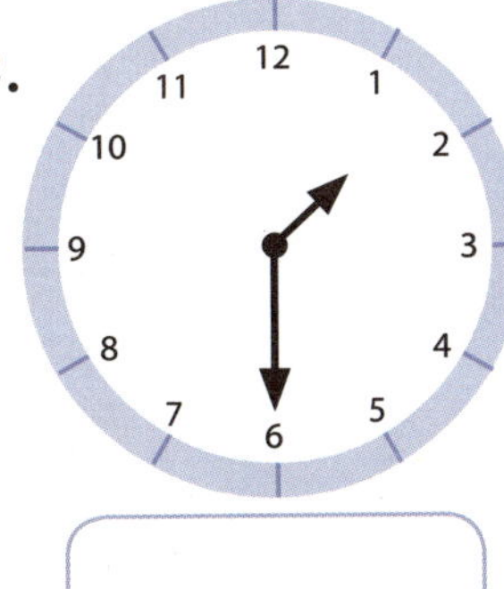

d. 

2. Draw the hands to show the time.

a. 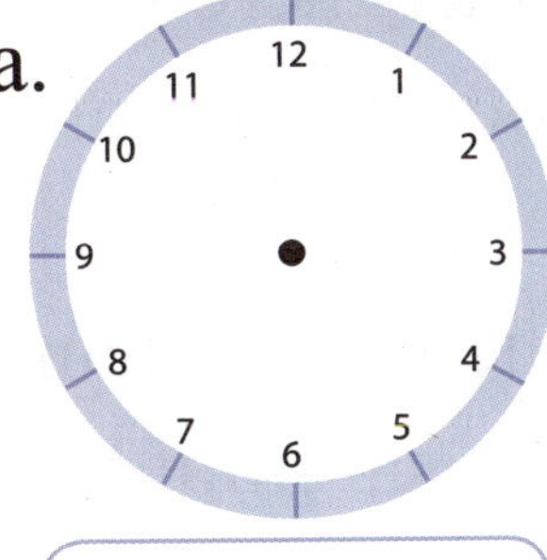

Half past 12

b. 

Half past 10

c. 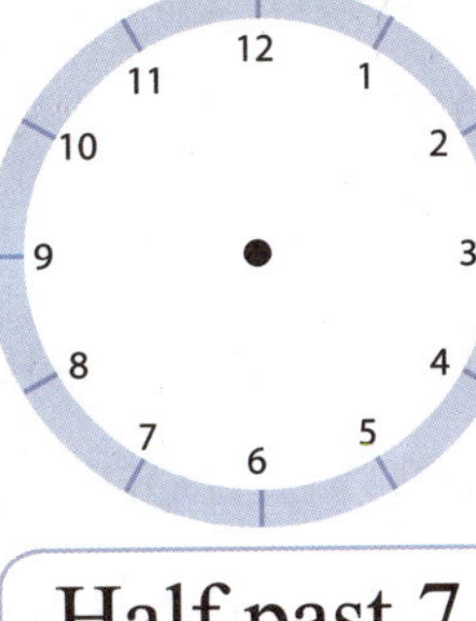

Half past 7

d. 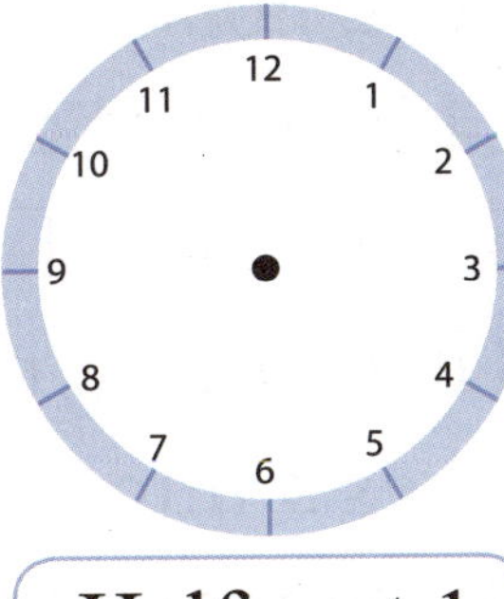

Half past 1

3. Draw minute and hour hands as told.

a. 

.... o' clock

2 hours later →

b. 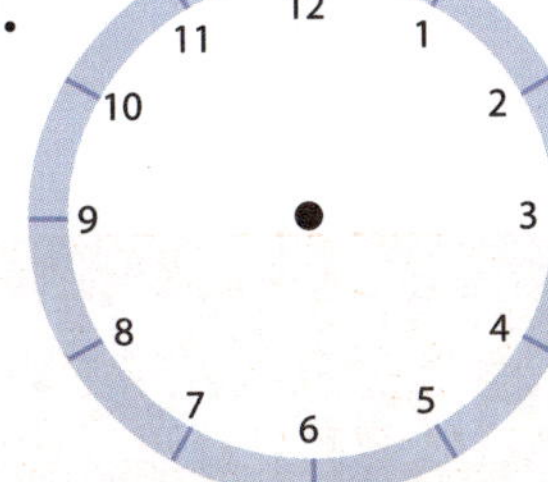

.... o' clock

3 hours later →

c. 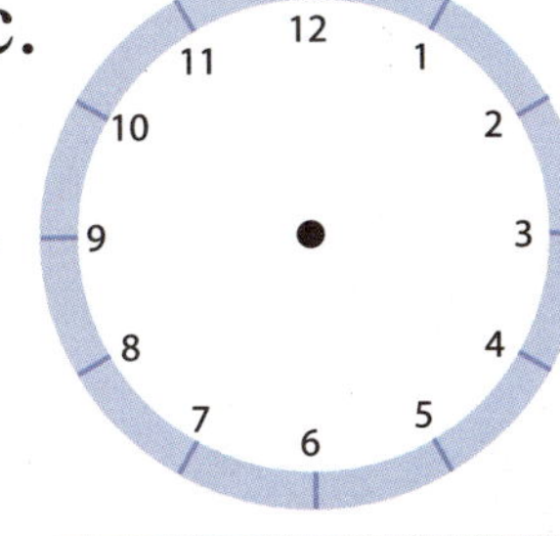

.... o' clock

4. Jenny fell asleep at half past 11. She slept for 2 hours. When did she get up? Show on the clock.

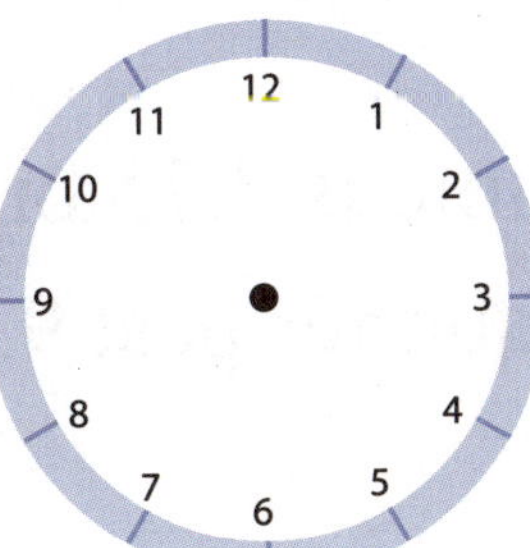

5. Jack had his lunch 1 hour back. Present time is shown in the clock below.

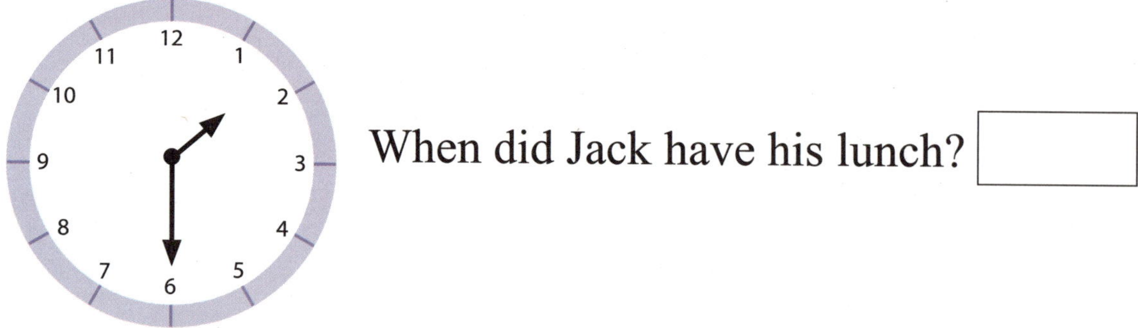

Reading Time

In 12 hours the hour hand goes all around the clock. In a day there are 24 hours. The hour hand makes 2 rounds in 1 day. In 1 hour the minute hand makes 1 round. 1 hour has 60 minutes.

There are 12 numbers on the clock. To go from 12 to 1, the minute hand takes 5 minutes. To move from 1 to 2, the minute hand takes 5 minutes. So, to move from 12 to 2 the hand took 5+5=10 minutes.

To move from 12 to 3 it takes 15 minutes. 15 minutes is called **quarter of one hour**.

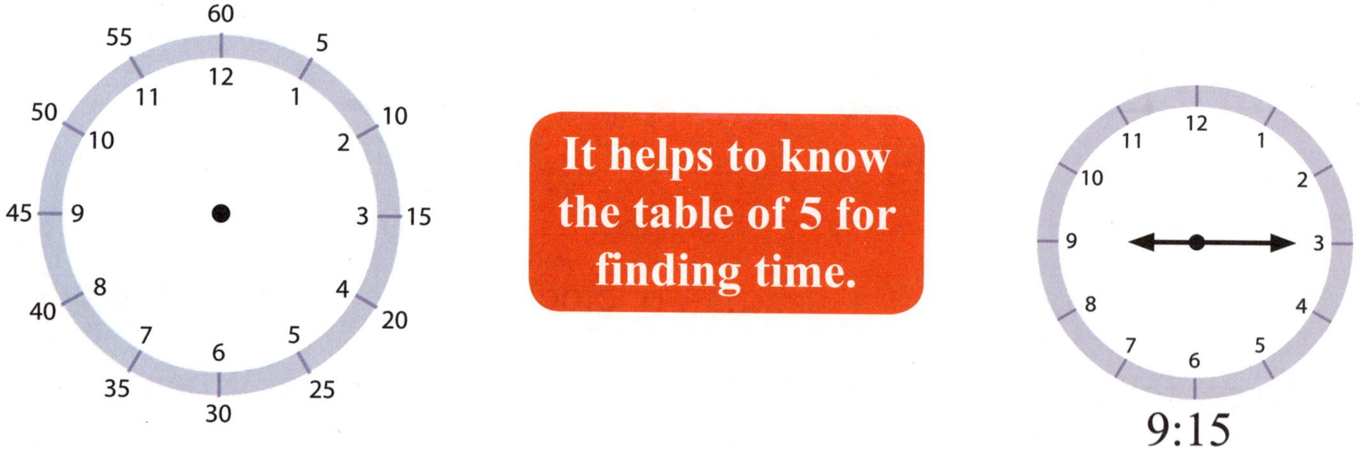

Quarter hour

When the minute hand is at 3, the hour hand is at 9, the time is 9:15 or 15 minutes past 9. 15 minutes is quarter of an hour. It is quarter past 9.

Quarter past 11

The hour hand is at 11 and minute hand is at 3

The time is 11:15 or 15 minutes past 11. It is also quarter past 11.

When the minute hand is at 3 time is read as quarter past.

Exercise 8.3

1. Look at the following clocks and write the correct time in both the ways as shown in the first one.

a. 4 : 15

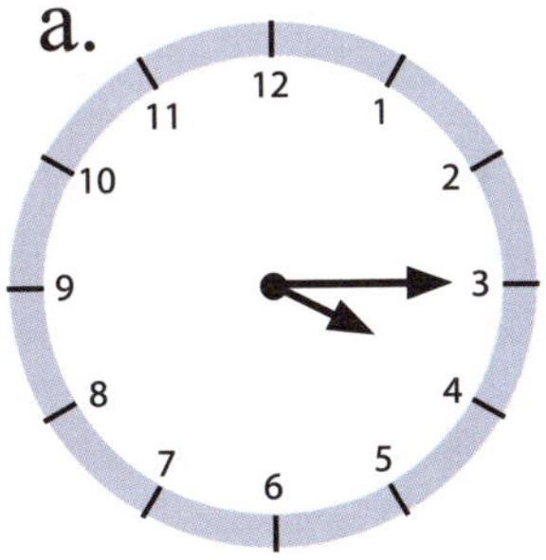

Quarter past 4

b.

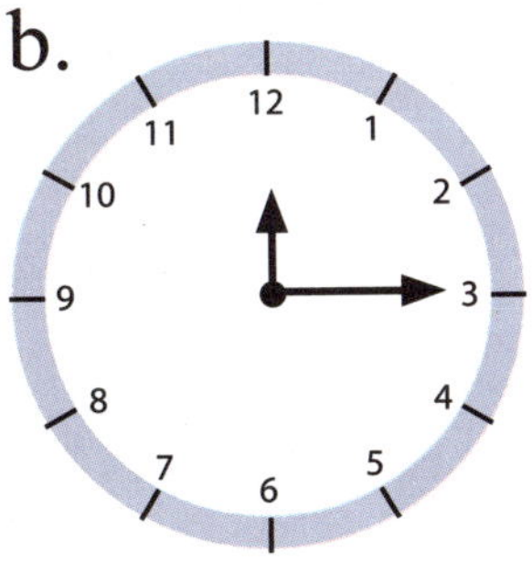

c.

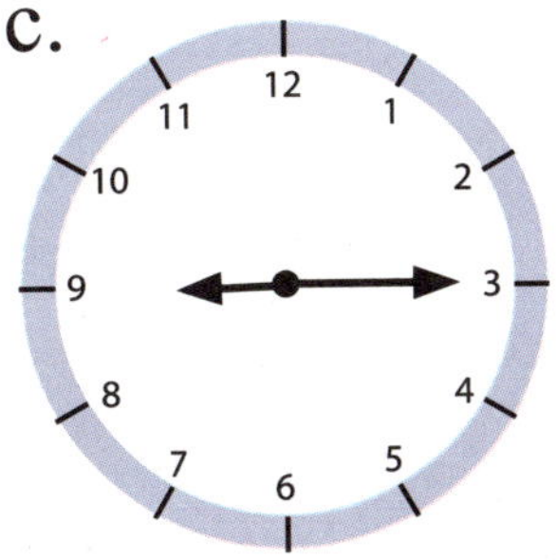

d.

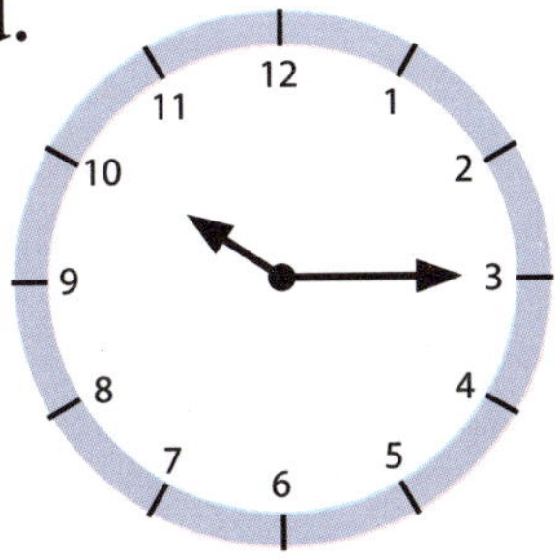

e.

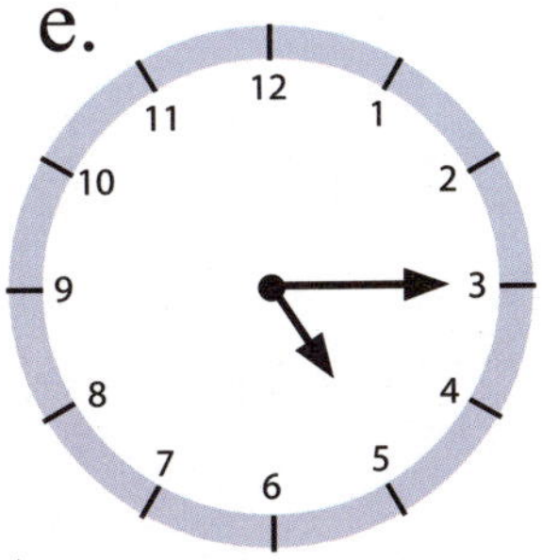

f.

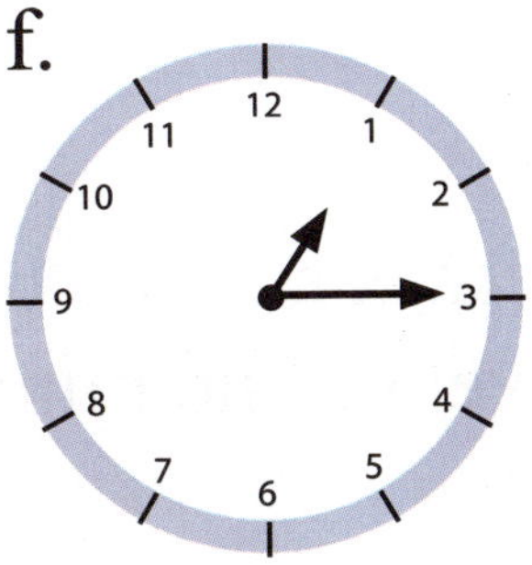

g.

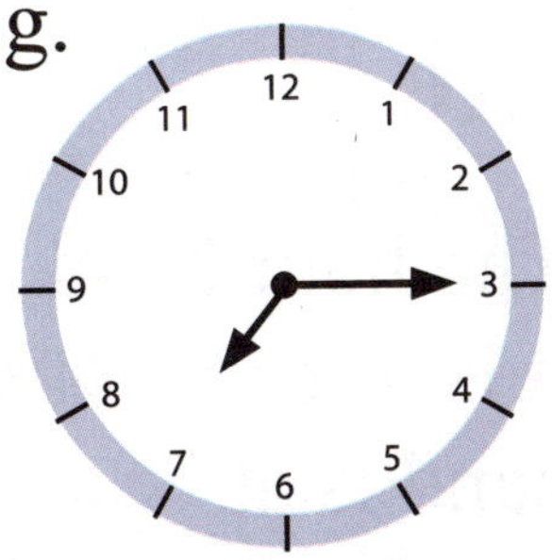

h.

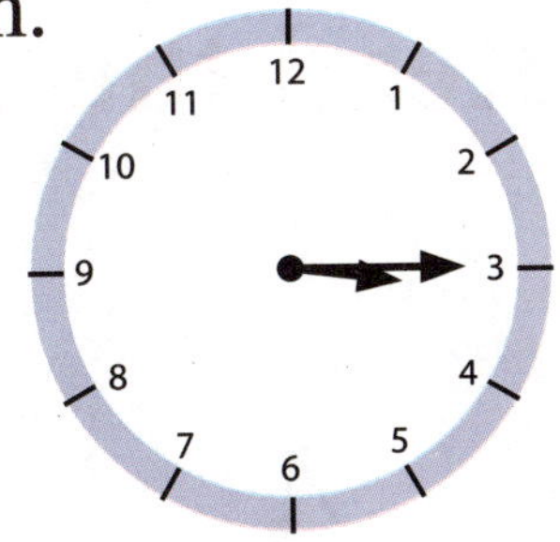

2. Draw the hands of the clock to show the time.

a. 10 : 15

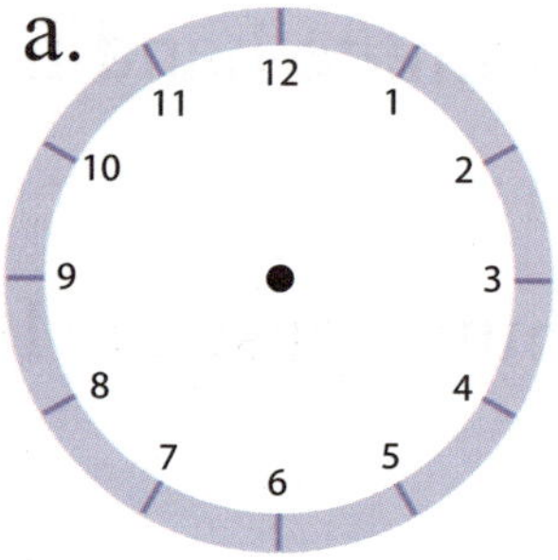

b. 1 : 15

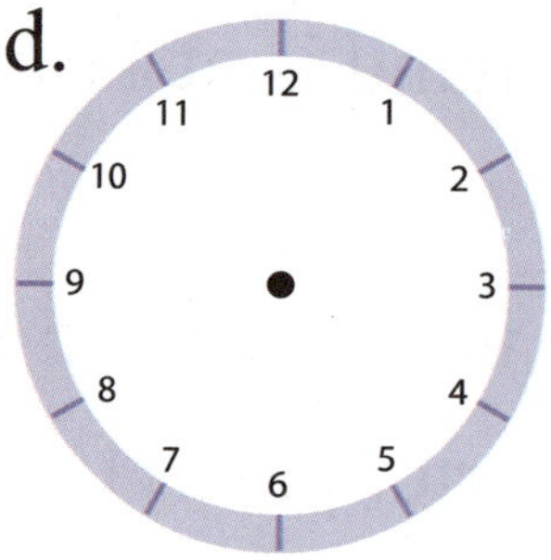

c. 12 : 15

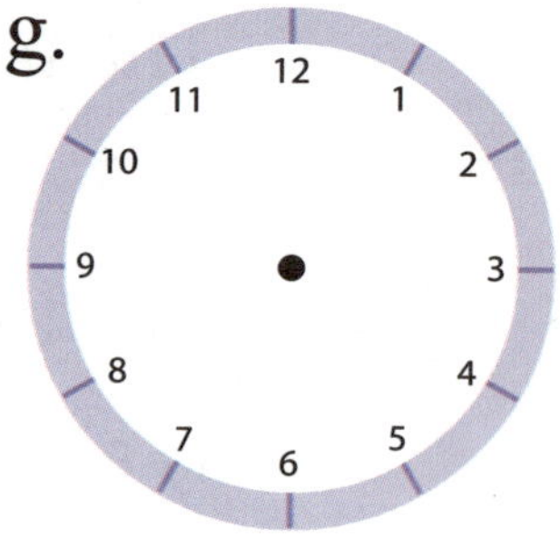

d. 7 : 15

e. 11 : 15

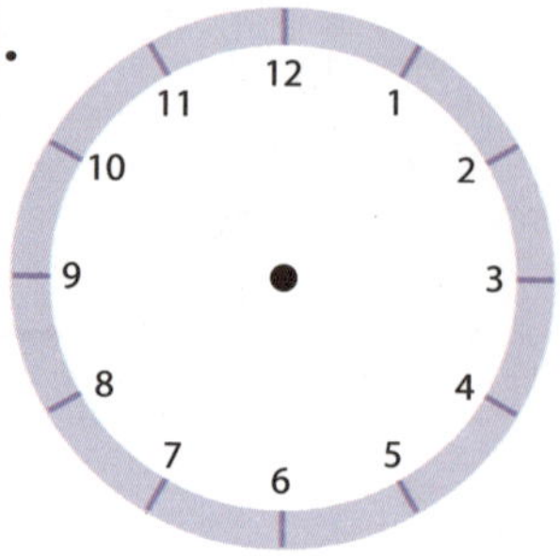

f. Quarter past 4

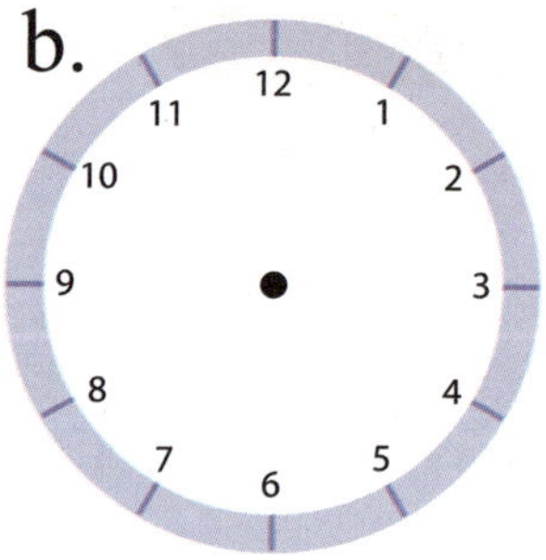

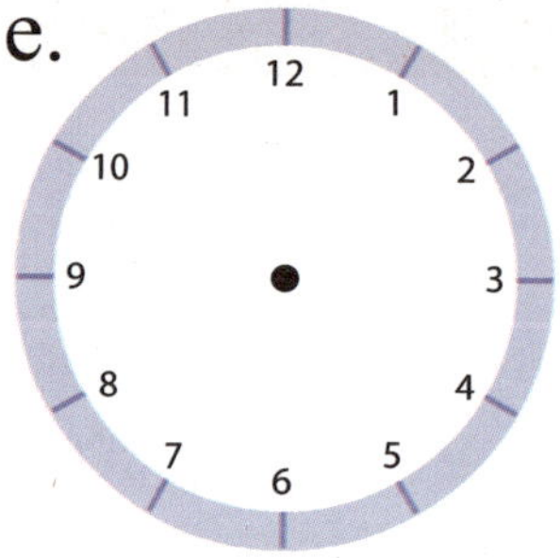

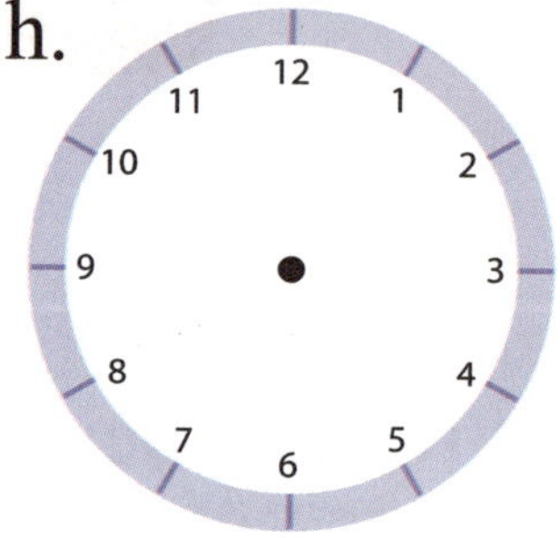

g. Quarter past 2

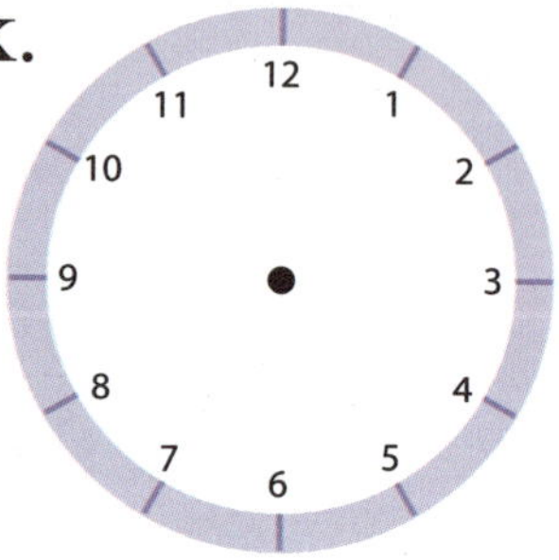

h. Quarter past 8

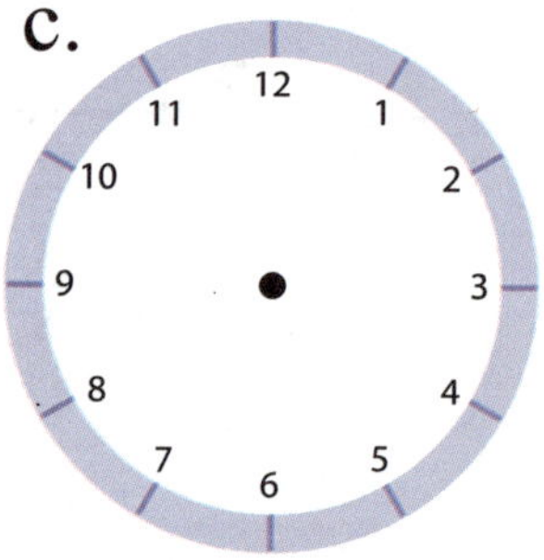

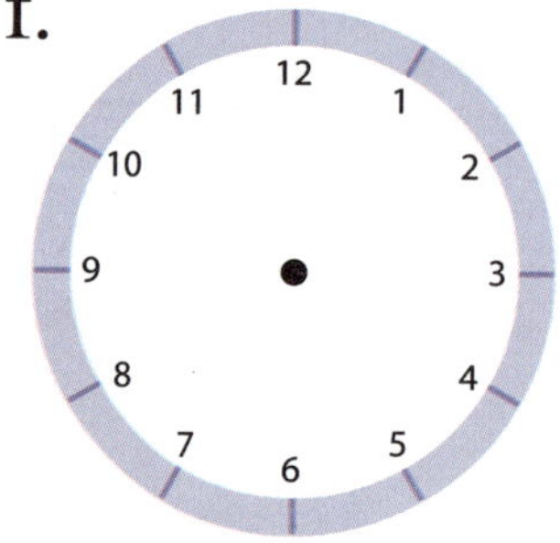

i. 5 : 15

j. 3 : 15

k. 9 : 15

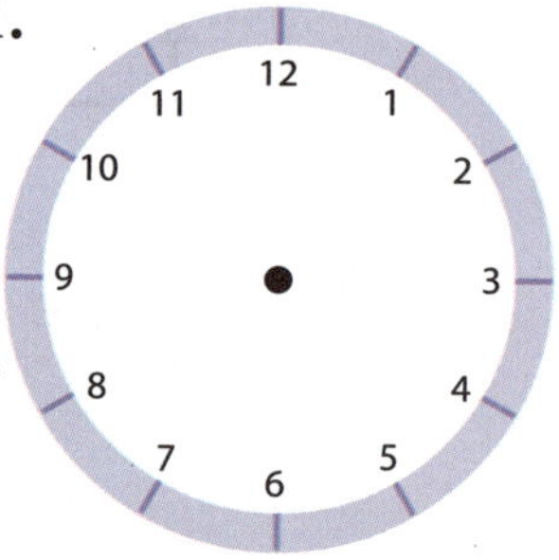

l. 6 : 15

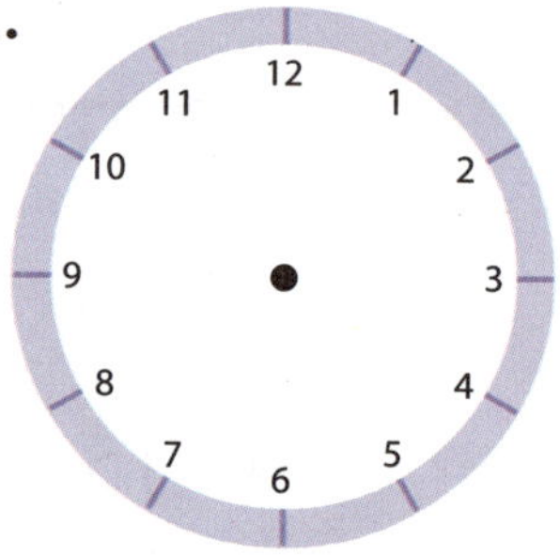

Read the Time

The hour hand is between 5 and 6. So, it is after 5 but not yet 6. The minute hand is at 7.

It is $7 \times 5 = 35$ minutes

Time is 5 : 35 or 35 minutes past 5

Lab Activity

Teacher should divide students into groups of 2 and give them clocks with movable hands.

1. What time is it?

7 : 50

50 minutes past 7

a.

b.

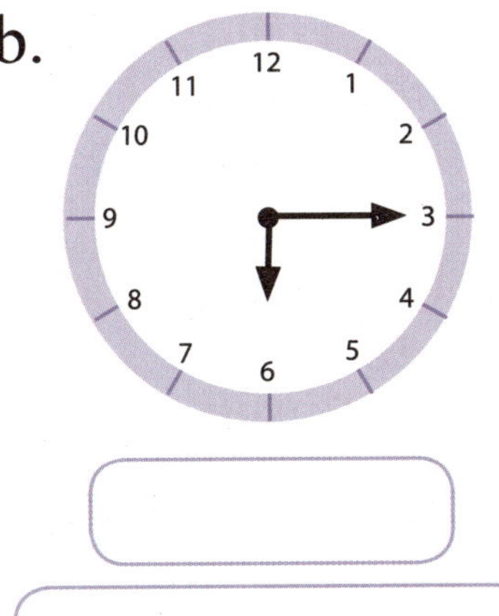

2. Draw the hands of the clock to show.

a.

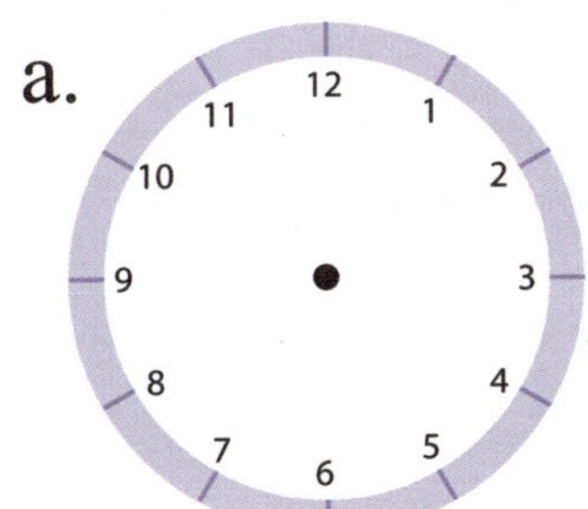

4 : 35

b.

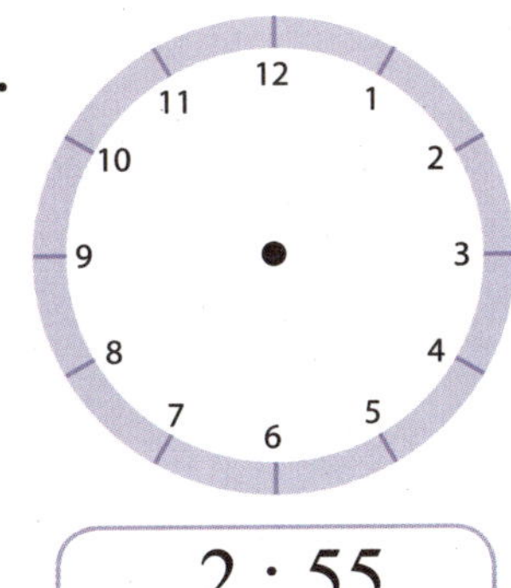

2 : 55

c.

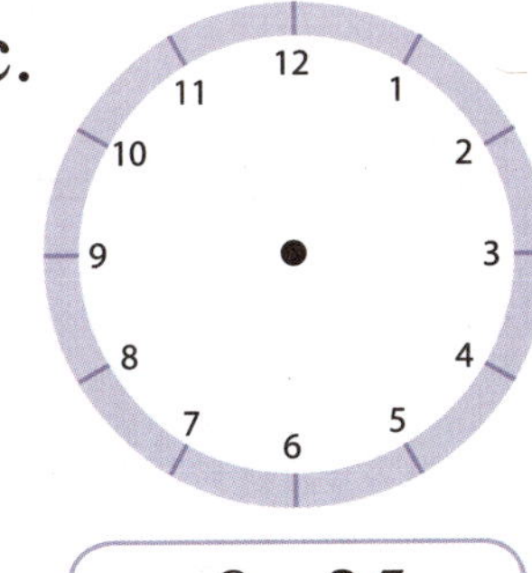

8 : 25

Days, Hours, Minutes

1 day = 24 hours

2 days = 24 + 24 = 2 × 24 hours = 48 hours

5 days = 5 × 24 = 120 hours

1 hour = 60 minutes

2 hours = 2 × 60 minutes

10 hours = 10 × 60 = 600 minutes

Exercise 8.4

1. Convert into hours as shown above.

a. 10 days = ____ d. 1 week = ____

b. 3 days = ____ e. 9 days = ____

c. 20 days = ____ f. 7 days = ____

2. Convert into minutes

a. 5 hours = ____ d. 8 hours = ____

b. 20 hours = ____ e. 1 day = ____

c. 15 hours = ____ f. 12 hours = ____

3. Convert into days

a. 3 weeks ____ days

b. 2 weeks 5 days = ____ days

4. Write True or False

a. 1 week = 6 days

b. 1 hour = 60 seconds

c. 60 minutes = 1 second

Calendar 2016 activity

Look at the calendar given below. It tells us about the days and months that will come in the year 2016.
We all know that a year has 12 months. Some months have 30 days and some 31 days.

JANUARY

S	M	T	W	T	F	S
					1	2
3	4	5	6	7	8	9
10	11	12	13	14	15	16
17	18	19	20	21	22	23
24	25	26	27	28	29	30
31						

FEBRUARY

S	M	T	W	T	F	S
	1	2	3	4	5	6
7	8	9	10	11	12	13
14	15	16	17	18	19	20
21	22	23	24	25	26	27
28	29					

MARCH

S	M	T	W	T	F	S
		1	2	3	4	5
6	7	8	9	10	11	12
13	14	15	16	17	18	19
20	21	22	23	24	25	26
27	28	29	30	31		

APRIL

S	M	T	W	T	F	S
					1	2
3	4	5	6	7	8	9
10	11	12	13	14	15	16
17	18	19	20	21	22	23
24	25	26	27	28	29	30

MAY

S	M	T	W	T	F	S
1	2	3	4	5	6	7
8	9	10	11	12	13	14
15	16	17	18	19	20	21
22	23	24	25	26	27	28
29	30	31				

JUNE

S	M	T	W	T	F	S
			1	2	3	4
5	6	7	8	9	10	11
12	13	14	15	16	17	18
19	20	21	22	23	24	25
26	27	28	29	30		

JULY

S	M	T	W	T	F	S
					1	2
3	4	5	6	7	8	9
10	11	12	13	14	15	16
17	18	19	20	21	22	23
24	25	26	27	28	29	30
31						

AUGUST

S	M	T	W	T	F	S
	1	2	3	4	5	6
7	8	9	10	11	12	13
14	15	16	17	18	19	20
21	22	23	24	25	26	27
28	29	30	31			

SEPTEMBER

S	M	T	W	T	F	S
				1	2	3
4	5	6	7	8	9	10
11	12	13	14	15	16	17
18	19	20	21	22	23	24
25	26	27	28	29	30	

OCTOBER

S	M	T	W	T	F	S
						1
2	3	4	5	6	7	8
9	10	11	12	13	14	15
16	17	18	19	20	21	22
23	24	25	26	27	28	29
30	31					

NOVEMBER

S	M	T	W	T	F	S
		1	2	3	4	5
6	7	8	9	10	11	12
13	14	15	16	17	18	19
20	21	22	23	24	25	26
27	28	29	30			

DECEMBER

S	M	T	W	T	F	S
				1	2	3
4	5	6	7	8	9	10
11	12	13	14	15	16	17
18	19	20	21	22	23	24
25	26	27	28	29	30	31

Months having 30 days: April, June, September, November

Months having 31 days: January, March, May, July, August, October, December

Close your fist. Start counting from the first month January from the first knuckle, February in the dip, March again in the knuckle and so on. The months on the knuckles have 31 days and the months in the dip have 30 days.

February has 28 days in normal years but 29 days in a leap year. It is the shortest month.

1 week = 7 days

EXAMPLE

5 weeks = 5 × 7 = 35 days

1 month = 30 days

1 year = 365 days

1 Leap year = 366 days

Exercise 8.5

1. Convert into days (1 month = 30 days, 1 week = 7 days)

a.	8 weeks	=	☐	d.	10 weeks	=	☐
b.	4 weeks	=	☐	e.	3 months	=	☐
c.	6 months	=	☐	f.	10 months	=	☐

2. Write these dates in the order in which they come in the year.

18th July (Nelson Mandela's Birthday) a. ______________________

4th July (American Independence Day) b. ______________________

1st May (Labour Day) c. ______________________

25th December (Christmas) d. ______________________

20th November (Universal Children's Day) e. ______________________

3rd May (Teacher's Day) f. ______________________

3. The school closed on 20th May, 2016 for 1 month and 15 days.

When will the school re-open?

____

4. Sam is 5 years younger than Jenny. Jenny was born in 2004.

When was Sam born?

____

5. Calendar Fun (An animation)

June 2016						
S	M	T	W	T	F	S
			1	2	3	4
5	6	7	8	9	10	11
12	13	14	15	16	17	18
19	20	21	22	23	24	25
26	27	28	29	30		

* Holiday

If you add numbers along the line see what you will get

a. $3 + 11 + 19 =$ ☐ b. $17 + 11 + 5 =$ ☐

c. $10 + 11 + 12 =$ ☐ d. $4 + 11 + 18 =$ ☐

What do you observe?
Yes, the answer in all cases is the same.

Mental Math

1. A movie started at 4:30 p.m. and got over after 2 hours 15 minutes. It means the show got over at _______ p.m.
2. 2 weeks = _______ days
3. If day after tomorrow is Saturday, day before yesterday was _______.
4. If yesterday was Tuesday, day after tomorrow will be _______.
5. If Christmas in a particular year fell on Wednesday, then 31st of that month will be on _______ .
6. Ricky takes 20 minutes to walk to school. If he leaves his house at 7:45 a.m. he reaches his school at _______ a.m.
7. 1 year 7 months = _______ months
8. Quarter of an hour = _______ minutes
9. Sid sleeps for 8 hours. If he went to sleep at 9 o' clock in the night he got up at _______ o' clock in the morning.
10. When the minute hand is at _______, time is read as 'quarter past'.

Symmetry and Patterns

We enjoy looking at flowers, butterflies and different shapes. We see that if a line is drawn in between, the two parts match perfectly.

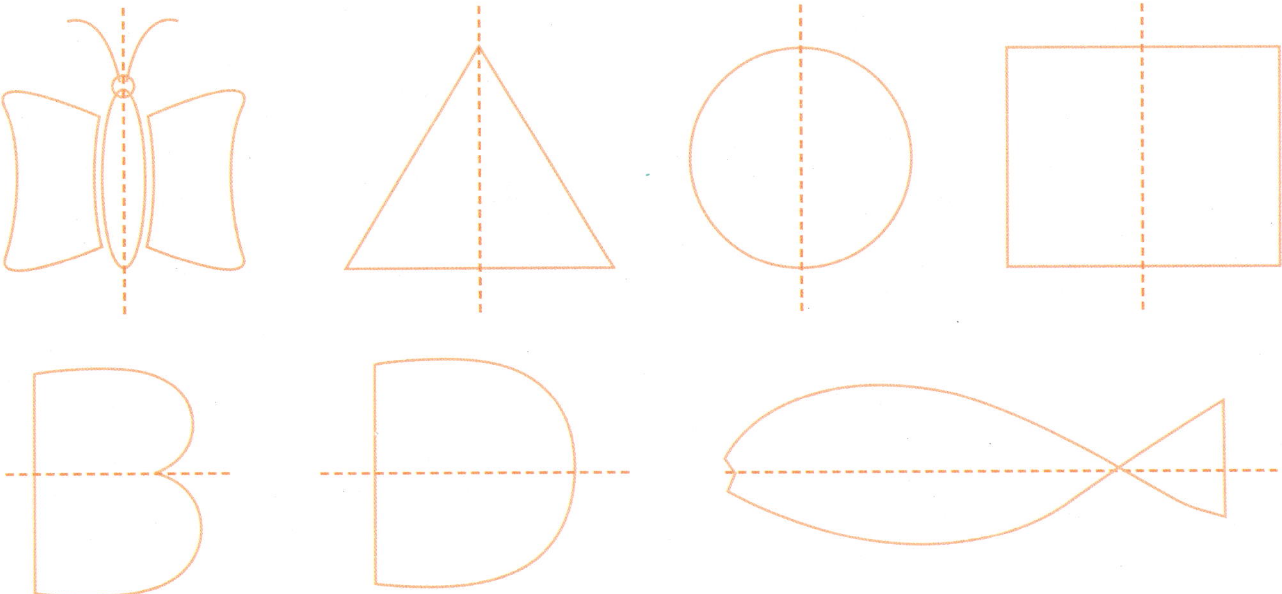

The dotted line is called the line of symmetry. In these figures, one part overlaps the other part exactly and these are symmetrical figures.

If we place a mirror along the dotted line, the other half of the shape can be seen.

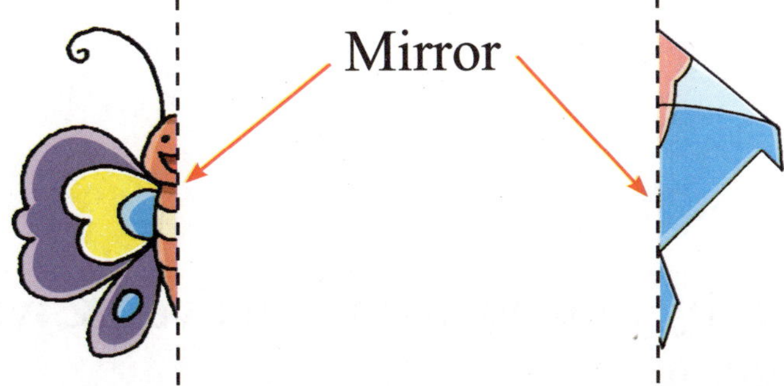

The figure inside the mirror and outside the mirror is the same. The two together form a complete shape.

The line of symmetry divides an object or a shape into two mirror halves.

Exercise 9.1

1. Tick (✓) the figures which are divide into two mirror halves by the dotted lines.

a. 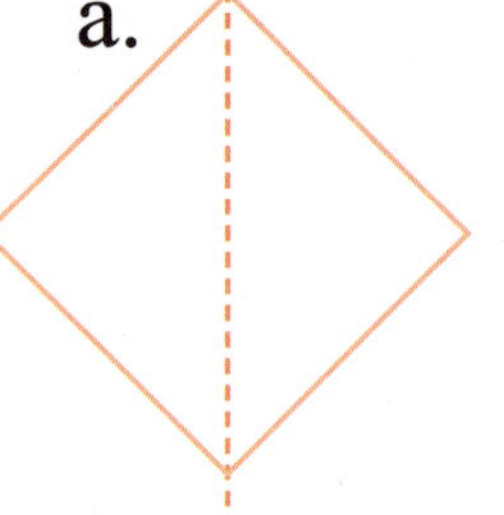

b. 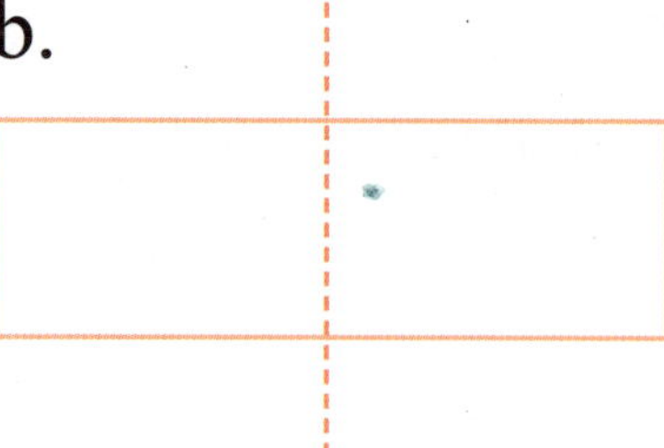

c. 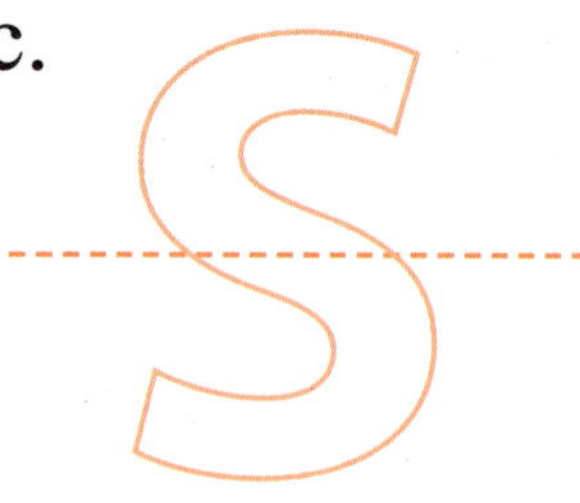

d. 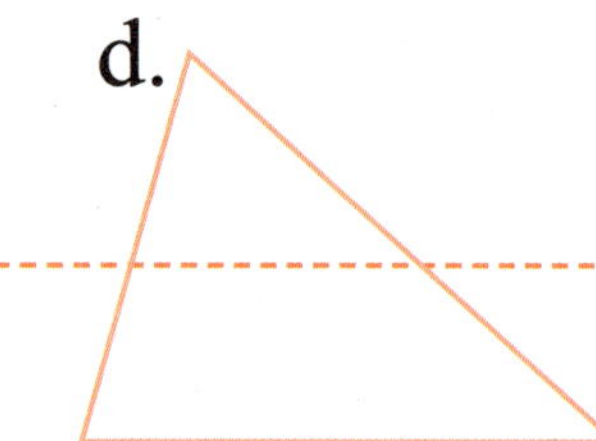

e. 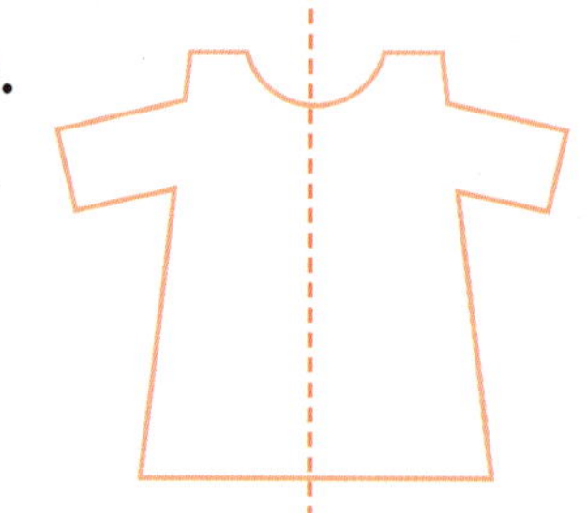

f. 

2. Using a dotted line divide the following pictures into mirror halves.

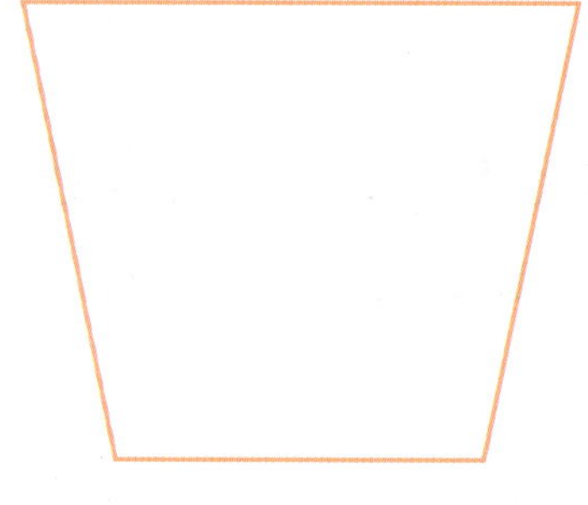

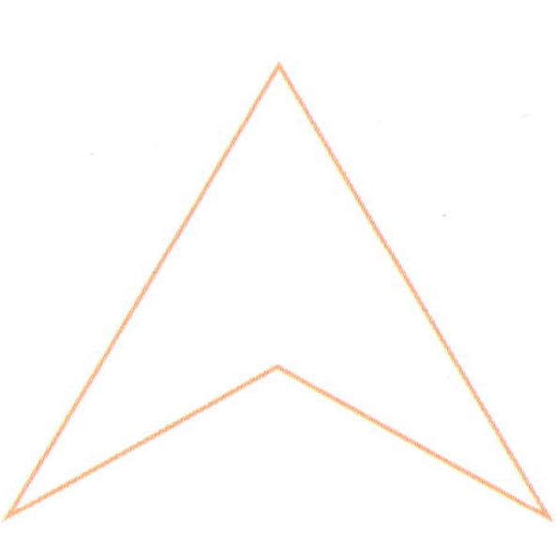

3. Guess each of the letter/words by looking at their halves & write them in the space provided below.

____________ ____________ ____________

Patterns

Understand the patterns & complete the rows.

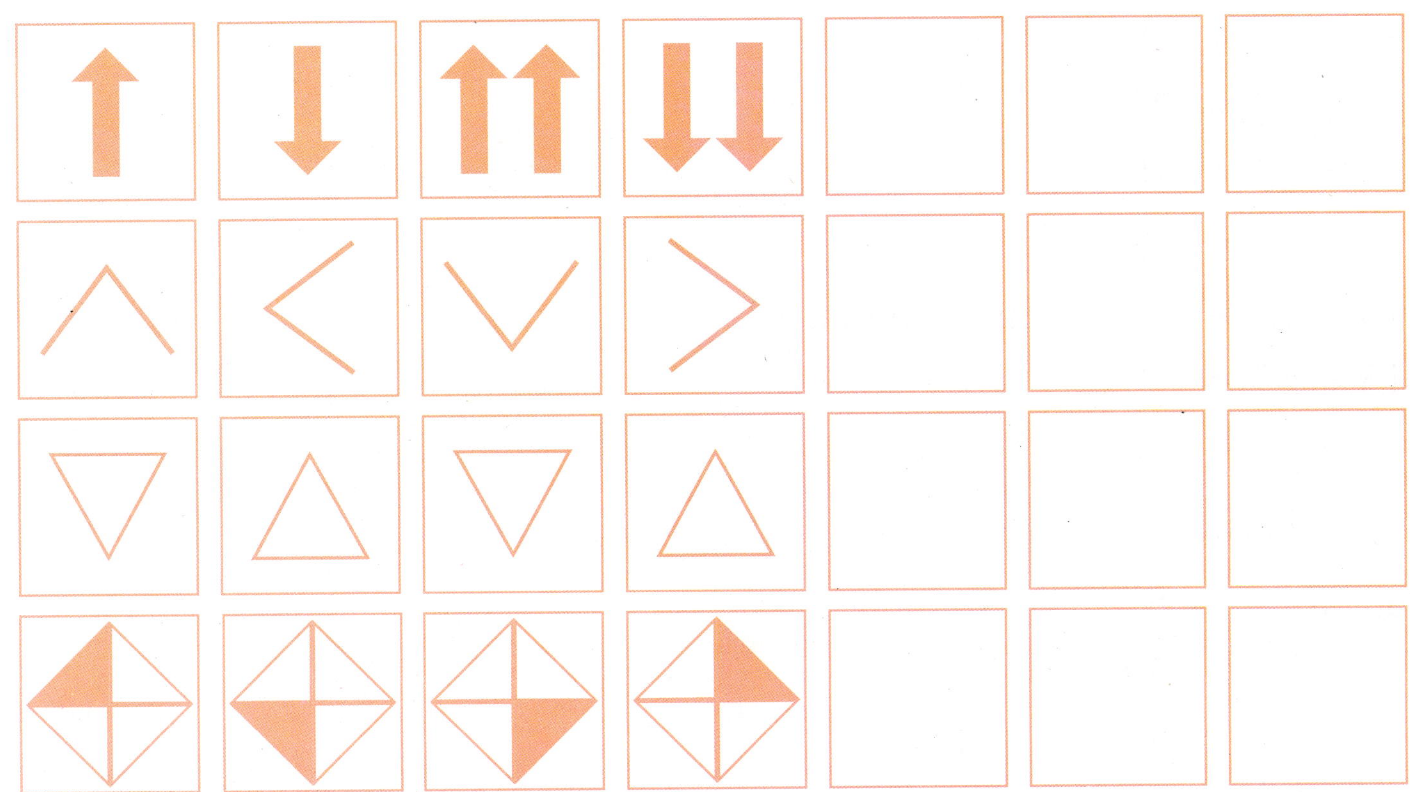

Follow the pattern and write the next numbers.

20	40	80	160			
700	600	500				
850	750	650				
2000	1950	1900				

We see patterns every where around us in numbers & designs.

Look at these interesting number patterns.

13 + 5 = 18

13 + 15 = 28

13 + 25 = 38

13 + 35 = 48

13 + 45 = ☐ Can you guess?

13 + 55 = ☐

4. Follow the pattern and write the next number.

a. 8 – 5 = 3

80 – 50 = 30

800 – 500 = 300

8000 – 5000 = ☐

b. 37 × 3 = 111

37 × 6 = 222

37 × 9 = 333

37 × 12 = ☐

37 × 15 = ☐

37 × 18 = ☐

Just follow the pattern! Do not multiply.

c. 1 × 1 = 1

11 × 11 = 121

111 × 111 = 12321

1111 × 1111 = ☐

11111 × 11111 = ☐

10 Money

We need money to purchase things. The currency used in the United States is Dollars and cents.
1 dollar = 100 cents.

Dollar = $
Symbol of Dollar = $, Cents = ¢

$ 2 = 2 × 100 = 200 cents

$ 7 = 7 × 100 = 700 cents

Dollar 8 and 50 cents

= 8 × 100 cents + 50 cents

= 800 + 50 cents

= 850 cents

There is a short form for writing seven dollars 60 cents = $ 7.60
Thirteen dollars 25 cents = $ 13.25
Twenty dollars 70 cents = $ 20.70
55 cents = $ 0.55
30 dollars 5 cents = $ 30.05 $ ~~30.5~~

Conversion of cent into dollar

EXAMPLE

1. 1500 cents = $ 15.00
2. 2385 cents = $ 23.85

Put a '.'after 2 digit from last (right)

Exercise 10.1

1. Fill in the blanks.

Money	In short form	In words
Dollars 50 and 30 cents	$ 50.30	
Dollars 26 and 15 cents		
6 cents		
Dollars 72 and 20 cents		

2. Convert into cents

a. $ 80
b. $ 13
c. $ 70.70
d. $ 125
e. 18 dollars 4 cents
f. $ 0.90
g. $ 21.25
g. $ 56

3. Convert into dollars

a. 375 ¢
b. 3000 ¢
c. 1200 ¢
d. 2025 ¢
e. 680 ¢
f. 6075 ¢
g. 1001 ¢
h. 990 ¢
i. 7210 ¢

Addition and subtraction of money

Money is added and subtracted in the same way, as in numbers.

EXAMPLE

Add $ 25.75 and $ 34.25

	$		¢
	25 (carry 1 1)	.	75 (carry 1)
+	34	.	25
	60	.	00

We cannot write 100 ¢ after the '.' So, 1 is carried over to dollars.

It is important to write the dot or decimal'.' one below the other.

EXAMPLE

Subtract $ 95.50 from $ 106.75

	$		¢
	106	.	75
−	95	.	50
	11	.	25

EXAMPLE

Find the difference

	$		¢
	1̸3̸5 (2 14)	.	1̸0 (9)
−	96	.	85
	38	.	15

Exercise 10.2

1. Add

a.
$		¢
34	.	28
+ 62	.	95

d.
$		¢
169	.	28
+ 76	.	95

g.
$		¢
327	.	85
+256	.	75

j.
$		¢
666	.	66
+777	.	77

b.
$		¢
100	.	45
+ 32	.	65

e.
$		¢
81	.	50
+147	.	35

h.
$		¢
295	.	55
+ 68	.	82

k.
$		¢
2000	.	20
+ 20	.	80

c.
$		¢
352	.	69
532	.	96
+325	.	99

f.
$		¢
482	.	35
541	.	82
+412	.	80

i.
$		¢
254	.	29
105	.	56
+425	.	90

l.
$		¢
125	.	50
521	.	60
+251	.	70

2. Add

a. $ 130.40, $ 96.55, $ 9.55

b. $ 1000.10, $ 100.10, $ 1.10

c. $ 29.95, $ 129.95, $ 1029.95

d. $ 7.75, $ 177.50, $ 1177.75

e. $ 85.50, $ 5.80, $ 0.80

3. Find the difference.

a.

$	¢
200	. 42
−190	. 35

b.

$	¢
80	. 48
− 28	. 49

c.

$	¢
67	. 17
− 7	. 68

d.

$	¢
638	. 70
−180	. 95

4. Subtract

a. $ 118.75 from $ 120

b. $ 333.33 from $ 600

c. $ 66.65 from $ 130.75

d. $ 252.95 from $ 253.15

e. $ 18.90 from $ 21.30

Word Problems

Example: Sandra has $ 42.60 in her piggy bank. Her mother gives her $ 5 more. How much money does Sandra have in her piggy bank now?

Solution:

Money Sandra has	=	$ 42.60
Her mother gives	=	$ 5.00
Total money	=	$ 47.60

Example: Ron has \$ 5. He spends \$ 3.60 on a burger? How much money is left with him?

Solution: Money Ron has = \$ 5

Money he spends on a burger = \$ 3.60

Money left with Ron = \$ 5 – ₹ 3.60

\$ 5.00
– \$ 3.60
\$ 1.40

\ Money left with Ron is \$ 1.40

Exercise 10.3

1. I bought sandals for \$ 12, a top for \$ 7 and ice cream for \$ 2. How much did I spend altogether?
2. A man bought a pen and paid \$ 2. He got back \$ 1.50 from the shopkeeper. How much did the pen cost him?
3. Harry has \$ 316.80. John has \$ 243.10. How much more money does Harry have?
4. David has \$ 5. How much more money does he need to buy a bat worth \$ 30?
5. Mr. Gomez bought 1 kg of sugar for \$ 3.50, 1 kg tea for \$ 15.50 and 1 kg rice for \$ 2.25. He gave a 50 dollar to the shopkeeper. How much money was returned to him?
6. Peter who is 13 years old, and his sister is 8 years old, go to the amusement park with their mother. How much does his mother pay for three tickets, if a ticket for above 12 years is \$ 2 and below 12 is \$ 1.
7. Harry bought stamps for \$ 0.50 and envelopes for \$ 1.60. How much did he spend in all?
8. Sam went to watch a movie. He paid \$ 10.00 for the tickets and spent \$ 5.60 on popcorn. He had taken \$ 50 for the movie. How much money is left with him after watching the movie?

Lab Activity

Aim: Adding cents to make dollars

Materials required: Sheets of paper to make play money, dice.

Method: Students put coins under the paper and shade. They get copies of coins. In this way they make play money. Students are divided into group of 3-4. Two of them roll the dice and get the (as many) play coins of 10 ¢ and 50 ¢ from the teacher as the number rolled i.e. if they roll 1, they have to ask for number of equivalent coins of 10 ¢ or 50 ¢ to make $ 1.

A target amount is set and the group that reaches it first is the winner.

Conclusion: Students learn to convert bigger denominations into smaller.

Mental Math

1. Jasmine has 2 fifty-dollar bills, 2 twenty dollar bills, 5 20 dollar bills and 10 5 dollar bills. If she spends $ 175, money left with her is _______.
2. 425 ¢ = $ _______
3. $ 70 = _______ ¢
4. $ 82 and 800 ¢ = $ _______
5. 650 ¢ + 650 ¢ = $ _______
6. 505 ¢ + $ 5 = $ _______
7. $ 420 is $ _______ more than $ 375.25
8. 8690 ¢ _______ $ 86.09 (>, <, =)
9. $ 5.77 _______ 577 ¢ (>, <, =)
10. 1000 ¢ = $ _______

11 Measurement of Length

We use these for measuring lengths in our routine activities.

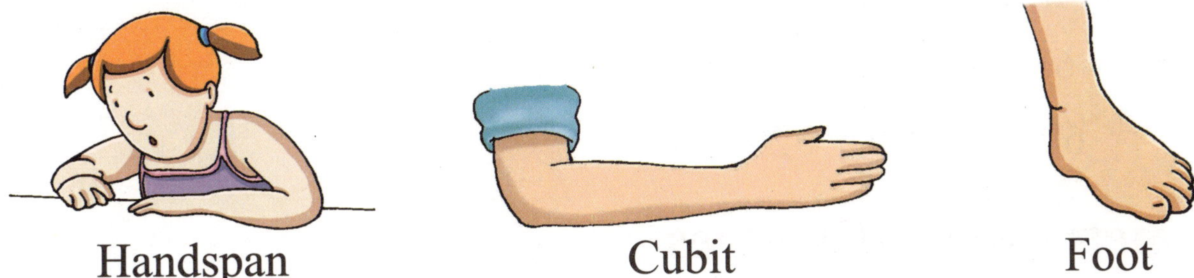

But there are certain standard units of length which are used universally.

Kilometre = km
Metre = m
Centimetre = cm
Millimetre = mm

A scale has cm, mm on one side and inches on the other.

1 m = 100 cm

Millimetre is a very small unit.

Kilometre is the bigger unit of measuring lengths.

ACTIVITY

Students can use their scale to measure different objects, their length, thickness and record it.

Object	Length	Thickness
Table		
Maths book		
Pencil box		
Pencil		
Eraser		

Kilometre

Distance is measured in kilometers (km)

1 km = 1000 m

5 km = 5 × 1000 m = 5000 m

6 km = 200 m = 6 × 1000 m + 200 m

6000 + 200 = 6200 m

Convert metre to centimetres

1 m = 100 cm

5 m = 5 × 100 = 500 cm

2 m 20 cm = 200 cm + 20 cm = 220 cm

Convert cm to mm

1 cm = 10 mm

3 cm = 30 mm

10 cm 5 mm = 10 × 10 mm + 5 mm

= 100 + 5 mm

= 105 mm

Exercise 11.1

1. Convert into metres

a. 6 km
b. 8 km 450 m
c. 3 km 950 m
d. 7 km 225 m

2. Convert into cm

a. 8 m
b. 3 m 70 cm
c. 10 m
d. 9 m 10 cm
e. 6 m
f. 7 m 75 cm

3. Fill in the boxes after conversion

a. 1 km = ☐ m

b. 1 m = ☐ cm

c. 3 km = ☐ m

d. 1 cm = ☐ mm

e. My pen is about ☐ long and my maths book is ☐ long

(25 cm, 10 cm)

Conversion of centimetre to metre

100 cm = 1 m

500 cm = 500/100 = 5 m

EXAMPLE

6000 cm = 6000/100 = 60 m

EXAMPLE

725 cm = 700 cm + 25 cm

= 700 ÷ 100 + 25 cm

= 7 m 25 cm

Conversion of metre to kilometre

1000 m = 1 km

4000 m = 4000 ÷ 1000 = 4 km

EXAMPLE

7525 m = 7000 m + 525 m

= 7000 ÷ 1000 + 525 m

= 7 km 525 m

Write the place value of the digits. The digit under thousands place gives km and the rest is metre

EXAMPLE

6819 m

Th	H	T	O
6	8	1	9 m
6 km	819 m		

Exercise 11.2

1. Fill in the blanks below.
   1. 600 cm = ___________ m
   2. 925 cm = ___________ m ___________ cm
   3. 1000 cm = ___________ m
   4. 150 cm = ___________ m ___________ cm
   6. 6 km = ___________ m
   7. 7 km = ___________ m
   8. 3 km 500 m = ___________ m + 500 m
   9. 8 km 880 m = ___________ m + ___________ m = ___________ m

Addition and subtraction.

1. Add 35 m 25 cm and 18 m 65 cm (Rules in columns)

	m	cm
	35	- 25
+	18	- 65
	53	- 90

Sum 53 m 90 cm

2. Subtract 26 m 50 cm from 50 m

	m	cm
	4 50 9	- 100
+	26	- 50
	23	- 50

Difference 23 m 50 cm

Exercise 11.3

1. Add

a. 58 m 35 cm; 6 m 25 cm

b. 69 m, 96 cm; 29 m, 38 cm

c. 75 m, 56 cm; 140 m, 39 cm

d. 139 m, 68 cm; 17 m, 9 cm, 24 m, 80 cm,

e. 33 m, 66 cm; 88 m, 82 cm

2. Subtract

1. 148 m 79 cm from 293 m 12 cm
2. 423 m 48 cm from 600 m 5 cm
3. 117 m 94 cm from 120 m 54 cm
4. 46 m 31 cm from 93 m 78 cm

3. Find the difference between the shortest and the longest ropes.

98 cm

63 cm

49 cm

4. Michael is 135 cm tall. He is 18 cm taller than Harry and 6 cm shorter than Paul. Who is shortest and find his height?
5. Every morning my father and I go jogging. He jogs for 850 m. He jogged 150 m more than me. How far did I jog?

Measurement of Mass

12

We know some objects are light and some objects are heavy. Why are objects light?

They are light because they weigh less. Some objects are heavy because their weight is more. Weight is actually mass in an object or a body. How can we know whether an object is heavy or light?

Actually by weighing

What do we use?

A weighing machine or a weighing scale

Different weighing machines for different objects.

Measures of weight

Most commonly used units are kilograms and grams.

1 kilograms (kg) = 1000 grams (g)

Gram (g) is used to weigh light objects, kilogram (g) is used to weigh heavy objects.

ACTIVITY

Teacher should give children different objects and ask them to guess if their weights will be in kg or g.

Exercise 12.1

1. Guess the weight nearest to the object mentioned from the following and circle it.

a.	An apple	70 g	7 g	7 kg
b.	A birthday cake	10 g	1 kg	100 kg
c.	Your Maths book	800 g	8 kg	8 g
d.	Feather	3 g	30 g	3 kg
e.	An egg	5 g	50 g	5 kg
f.	A man	70 kg	7 g	70 g

Conversion of kilogram into grams

1 kg = 1000 g

So, 3 kg = 3 × 1000 g = 3000 g

EXAMPLE

4 kg 275 g = 4 × 1000 g + 275 g
= 4000 g + 275 g
= 4275 g

EXAMPLE

8 kg 500 g = 8 × 1000 g + 500 g
= 8000 g + 500 g
= 8500 g

EXAMPLE

2 kg 60 g = 2 × 1000 g + 60 g
= 2060 g

Exercise 12.2

1. Convert into grams

a. 9 kg = 9 × 1000 g = 9000 g

b. 5 kg = ______ × ______g = ______g

c. 7 kg = ______ × ______g = ______g

d. 5 kg 800 g = 5 ______g + 800 g = ______g + 800 g = ______g

e. 3 kg 215 g = ____ × 1000 g + 215 g = ______g + 215 g = _____g

f. 6 kg 495 g = ______g + ______g = ______g + ______g = ____g

g. 8 kg 8 g = ______g + 8 g = ______g

h. 3 kg 30 g = ______g + ______g = ______g

Conversion of grams into kilograms

1000 g = 1 kg

2000 g = 2 kg

EXAMPLE

Example 1: 5000 g = 5000/1000 = 5 kg

Example 2: 6435 = 6000 g + 435 g

= 6000/1000+435 g

= 6 kg 435 g

Example 3: 2076 g = 2076 g = 2 kg 76 g

There is a simple method. If 4320 is written under the place value

Th	H	T	O
4	3	2	0

the digit in thousands place is the kg and rest are grams.

4 kg 320 g

Addition and Subtraction of Units of Mass

Add : 2 kg 500 g and 3 kg 50 g

	kg	g
	2	500
+	3	050
	5	550

Sum 5 kg 550 g

Subtract : 7 kg 200 g from 9 kg 150 g

	kg	g
	~~9~~ 8	1150
−	7	200
	1	950

Difference 1 kg 950 g

Important points to remember

1. 1 kg = 1000 g
   So, 3 digits willbe written under g, if 50g it willbe written 050 g.
2. Write in vertical columns
3. Add grams and then kg

Exercise 12.3

1. Convert into kilograms and grams

   a. 8000 g = _______kg _______g

   b. 5895 g = _______kg _______g

   c. 2900 g = _______kg _______g

   d. 6075 g = _______kg _______g

   e. 3365 g = _______kg _______g

2. Subtract by making sums.

   a. 12 kg from 25 kg 500 g

   b. 22 kg 225 g from 50 kg 150 g

   c. 25 kg 585 g from 30 kg

   d. 48 kg 275 g from 74 kg 50 g

   e. 50 kg from 50 kg 30 g

3. Write >, <, =

a.	3500 g		3 kg 50 g	b.	2775 kg		2 kg 575 g
c.	7082 g		7 kg 92 g	d.	9520 g		9 kg 250 g
e.	6902 g		6 kg 920 g	f.	8450 g		8 kg 450 g
g.	5148 g		5 kg 48 g	h.	4500 g		4 kg 6 g

4. Solve the following word problems.

a. Sylvia bought 5 kg 500 g of sugar and 3 kg 250 g of fruits. What was the total weight she was carrying?

b. A box of sweets weighed 4 kg 500 g. If the weight of the box is 600 g, what is the weight of the sweets?

c. Ricky weighed 53 kg and his brother weighed 8 kg 500 g less. What is his brother's weight?

d. A man was pulling a cart which had 20 kg 500 g of rice and 15 kg 750 g of wheat? What was the total weight?

e. 38 kg 500 g of potatoes was bought for a party. 19 kg 850 g was used. Find the weight of potatoes left.

Measurement of Capacity

13

Capacity of a container is the amount of liquid it can hold.

It is measured in milliliters and litres.

Millilitre (mL) is used to measure small amounts. Litres (L) is used to measure large amounts.

1 L= 1000 mL

Exercise 13.1

1. Fill in 'mL' or 'L' in the boxes to measure each.

   a. Liquid in a spoon ☐

   b. Water in a bucket ☐

   c. Juice in a cup ☐

   d. Shampoo is a sachet ☐

   e. Ink in a bottle ☐

   f. Water in swimming pool ☐

   g. Medicine in a bottle ☐

2. Circle the best option for the following.

a. A glass of milk	20 mL	2 L	2 mL
b. Your water bottle contains	25 L	250 L	500 mL
c. A teaspoon contains	5 mL	50 mL	5 L

ACTIVITY

Measurement of Capacity

Vessels which are larger in size will hold more liquid than vessels that are smaller in size.

A bucket has more capacity than a mug.

Liquids take the shape of the container in which they are kept.

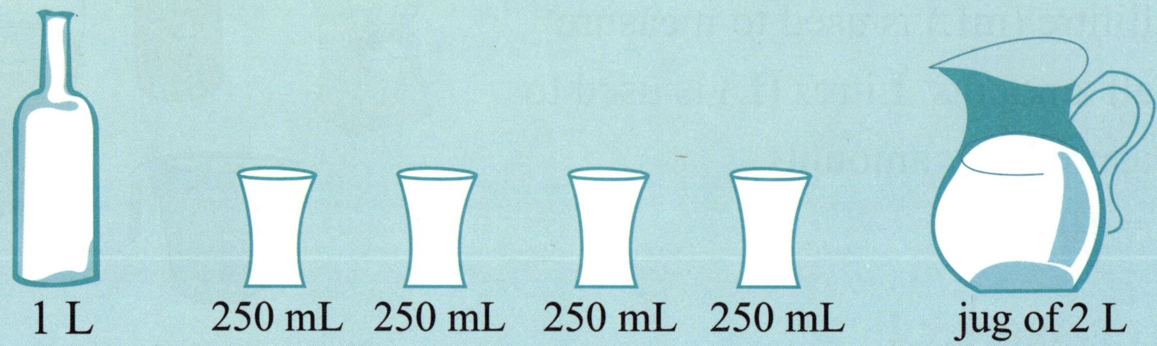

If four glasses are poured in the bottle, it will be full. Water takes the shape of glass then the shape of the bottle.

Let us perform this activity and then answer the following questions:-

1. How many children can have a glass of juice from the 1 L bottle? (Each glass = 250 mL)
2. How many bottles of juice will fill the jug?

Conversion of litres into millilitres

1 L= 1000 mL

2 L= 2 × 1000 mL= 2000 mL

4 L= 4 × 1000 mL= 4000 mL

(just like kg to g)

EXAMPLE

3 L 450 mL= 3000 mL+ 450 mL= 3450 mL

Conversion of millilitres to litres

1000 mL= 1 L

4000 mL= 4000/1000 mL= 4 L

1. 5845 mL= 5000 mL+ 845 mL

= 5000/1000 + 845 mL

= 5 L+ 845 mL

(Can be done in a simpler way) Write the place value, the digit in thousands place is the 'L' and the rest is 'mL'

ThHTO
7250 mL= 7 L 250 mL

Exercise 13.2

1. Convert into mL

   a. 6 L 250 mL= 6 × 1000 mL+ 250 mL= 6000 mL+ 250 mL= 6250 mL

   b. 8 L 125 mL= 8 × ______mL+ 125 mL= ______mL+ ______ mL= ______mL

   c. 7 L+ 555 mL= 7 × ______mL+ 555 mL= ______mL+ ______ mL= ______mL

   d. 4 L 28 mL= ______+ 28 mL

   e. 3 L 15 mL= ______mL

2. Convert to L into mL

   a. 7000 mL = ____________ L

   b. 8000 mL = ____________ L

   c. 6500 mL = ____________ L ____________ mL

   d. 2850 mL = ____________ L ____________ mL

   e. 1095 mL = ____________ L ____________ mL

   f. 6080 mL = ____________ L ____________ mL

   g. 9590 mL = ____________ L ____________ mL

3. Fill in the blanks.

a. 4 L= ______ mL

b. ______ L= 6000 mL

c. 3 L______ mL= 3750 mL

d. 7 L 354 mL= ______ mL

e. ______ L ______ mL= 5050 mL

f. ______ L= 9000 mL

g. ______ L______ mL= 6375 mL

h. 8______ = 8000 mL

Adding and subtracting L and mL

1. Add 5 L 225 mL and 8 L 885 mL (write in columns and add or subtract)

	L	mL
	5	225
+	8	885
	14	110

Sum 14 L 110 mL

2. Subtract 15 L 300 mLfrom 28 L 750 mL

	L	mL
	28	750
–	15	300
	13	450

Difference 13 L 450 mL

Exercise 13.3

1. Addition

a. 17 L 286 mL, 25 L 456 mL

b. 45 L 725 mL, 38 L 655 mL

c. 36 L 197 mL, 15 L 650 mL

d. 32 L 45 mL, 47 L 515 mL

e. 40 L, 38 L 20 mL, 7 L 176 mL

f. 50 L 215 mL, 18 L, 24 mL

2. Subtract

   a. 27 L 350 mL from 30 L 150 mL

   b. 15 L 500 mL from 25 L

   c. 13 L 127 mL from 25 L

   d. 8 L 80 mL from 31 L 3 mL

   e. 78 L 750 mL from 90 L 336 mL

3. Read the problems carefully and solve them.

   a. For a party my mother made 5 L 500 mL of juice. Only 3 L 380 mL was consumed. How much juice is left?

   b. 40 L 450 mL of water was put in the tank on Monday. On Tuesday 35 L 480 mL was added. How much water was there in the tank?

   c. To prepare custard for 20 people 6 L 20 mL milk is needed. Mother bought 7 L 50 mL. How much milk is left?

   d. To 2 L 200 mL of lemon concentrate 3 L 50 mL of water is needed. How much lemon juice is there?

Mental Math

1. 4538 cm = _______ m
2. _______ packets of 250 mL make 1 L
3. Capacity of a vessel is expressed in _______ or _______.
4. 7 kg = _______ g
5. A gas cylinder weighs 34 kg 450 g when full and 12 kg 500 g when empty. The weight of gas in the cylinder is _______.
6. 9 km 50 m = _______ m
7. A mango weighs 250 g. If Ricky buys 1 kg there will be _______ mangoes.
8. Danny was 1 m 35 cm tall. His height is _______ cm; his brother is 25 cm taller than him. So, his brother's height is _______ m.
9. Fill in with m, cm, km, g, kg, mL, L.
   a. Length of the pencil is 4 _______
   b. My text book weighs about 300 _______
   c. Capacity of an overhead tank is 1000 _______
   d. My mother's dress is 5 _______ long
   e. Distance between my home and school is 7 _______
   f. Capacity of my water bottle is 450 _______.

Geometry

14

In the previous classes we have seen flat shapes and solid shapes.

Let us explore some flat shapes

Figure	Name	Sides	Corners
side, corner	Rectangle	4	4
	Square	4	4
	Circle	0	0
	Triangle	3	3

Solids

Object	Name	Surface	Edges	Corners
	Cube	6 plane	12	8
	Cone	1 curved 1 plane	________	1
	Cyclinder	2 plane 1 curved	________	________
	Sphere	1 curved	0	0

Lab Activity

Teacher should encourage students to bring a solid shaped object (like a ball or a cube) to school. They should be placed in a box. It should have objects of different shapes.

Students should be given these objects, so that they can understand 'faces', 'edges', 'corners' of solids.

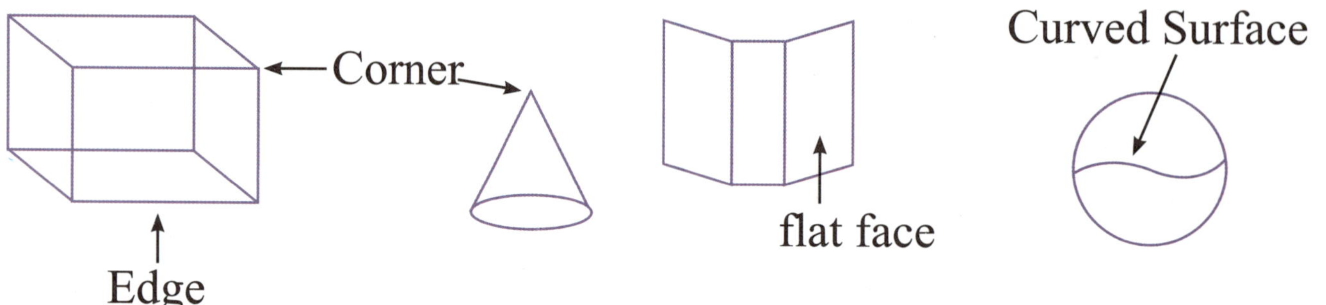

Exercise 14.1

1. Choose the correct answer from the options and fill in the blanks.

   a. A Christmas tree has the shape of a __________ and a straw has the shape of a __________ (cylinder, cone, sphere)

   b. A match box has the shape of a __________ and the chalk of a __________ (cylinder, cuboid, cube)

   c. The birthday cap is of the shape of __________ and the rolling pin is a __________ (cone, cube, cylinder)

   d. The egg has a __________ surface (curved, plane)

   e. Objects which have __________ surface slide and objects which have __________ surface roll. (Curved, plane)

2. Answer the following

   a. Name a fruit which has only curved surface.

   b. Name an object which has a plane surface and a curved surface.

Lab Activity

1. Draw a triangle by joining the dots.

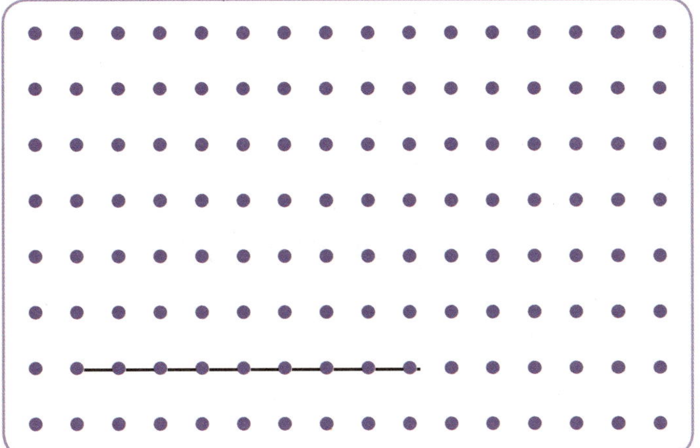

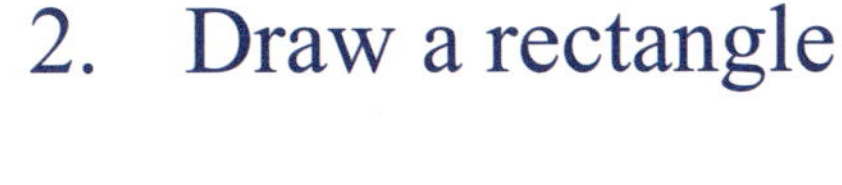

2. Draw a rectangle

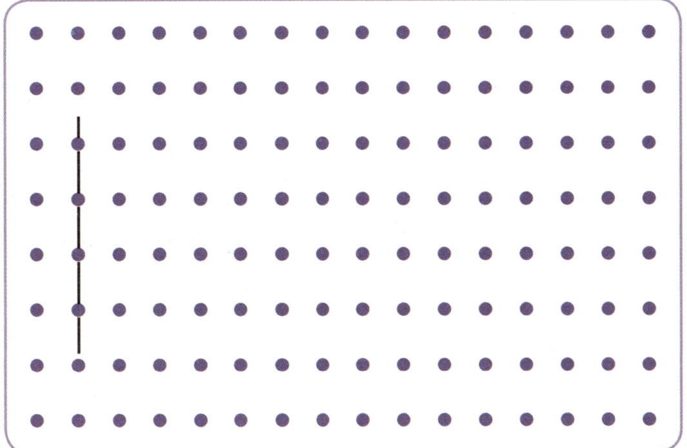

3. Draw a square

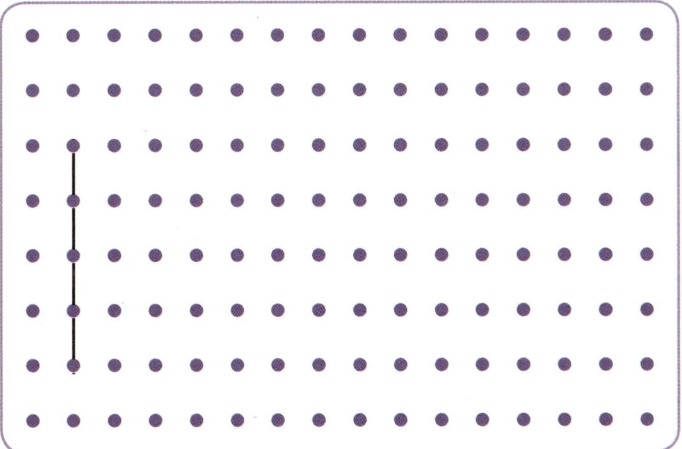

4. Draw a triangle

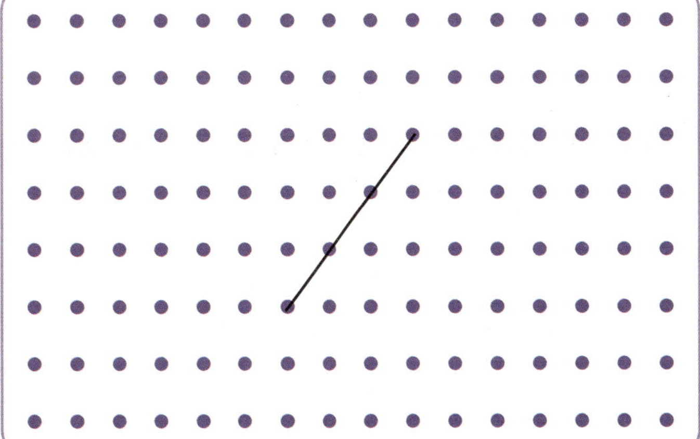

5. Draw lines to change into a rectangle.

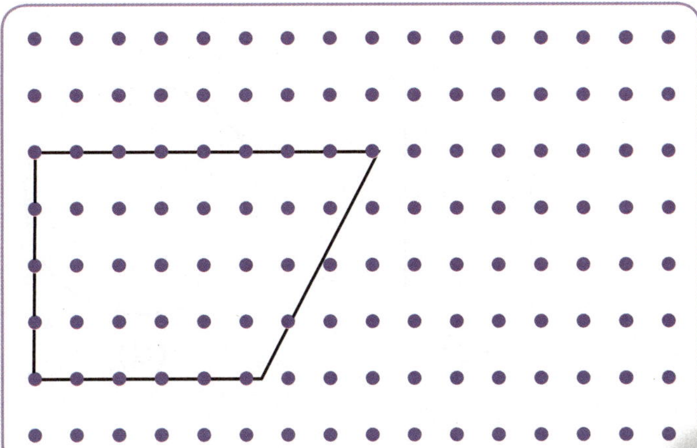

6. Draw lines to change into a rectangle.

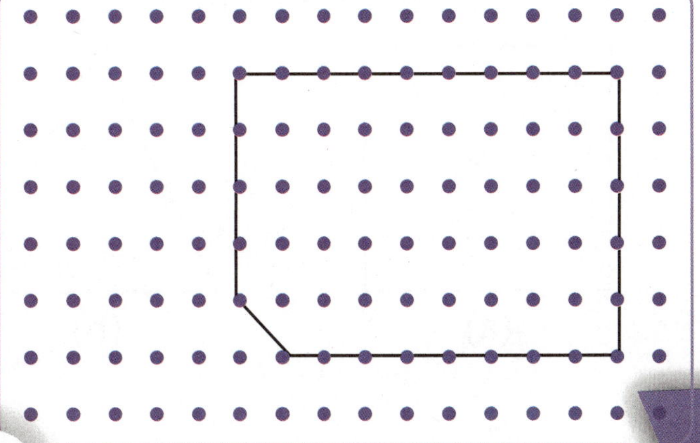

Types of Lines

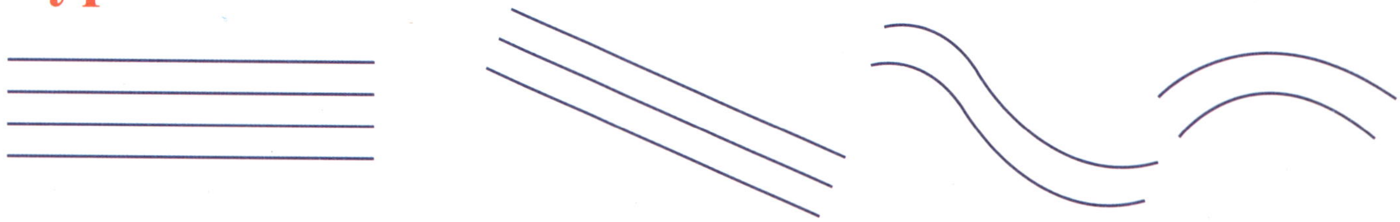

Straight lines

Curved lines

A triangle, rectangle and square are made of straight lines

A circle is made of a curved line

Open and Closed Figures

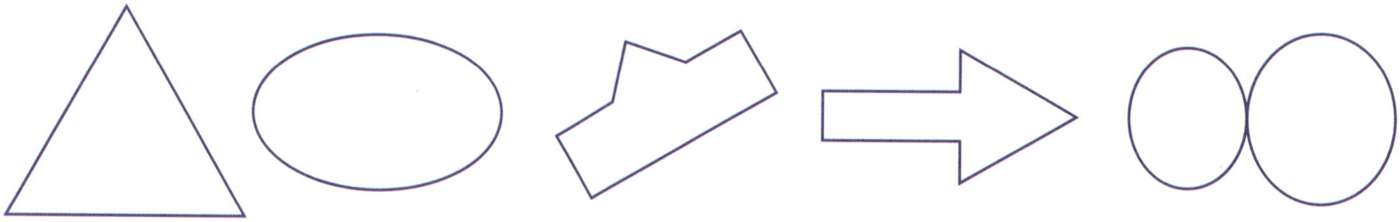

Each of above figures is a closed figure.

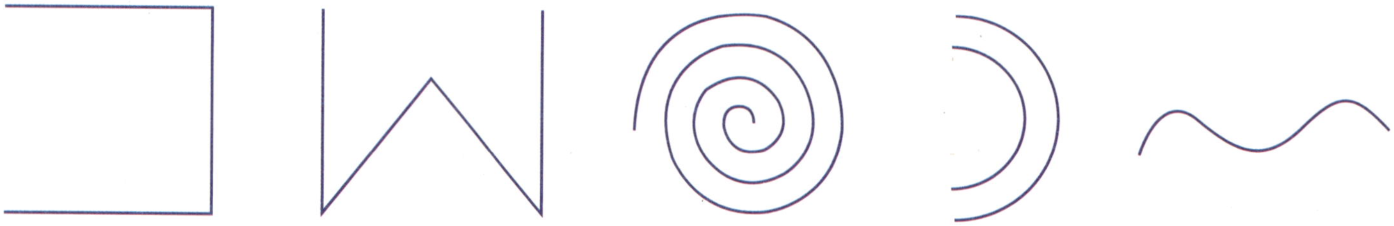

Each of these is an open curve

Exercise 14.2

1. Write the names of these figures

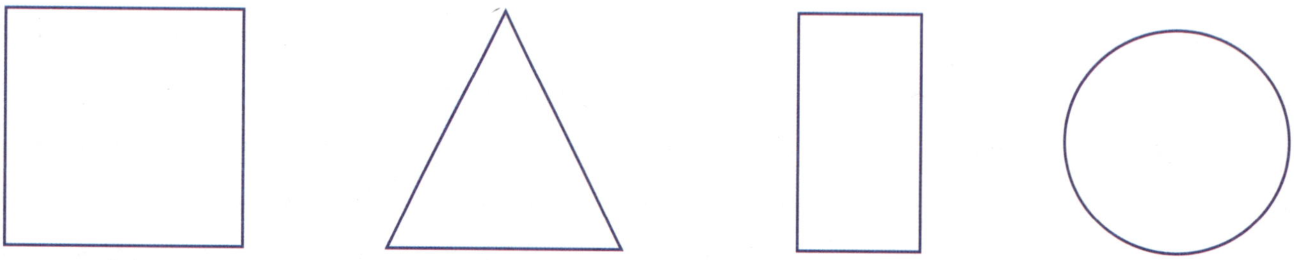

(a) (b) (c) (d)

2. Identify the following figures as open or closed.

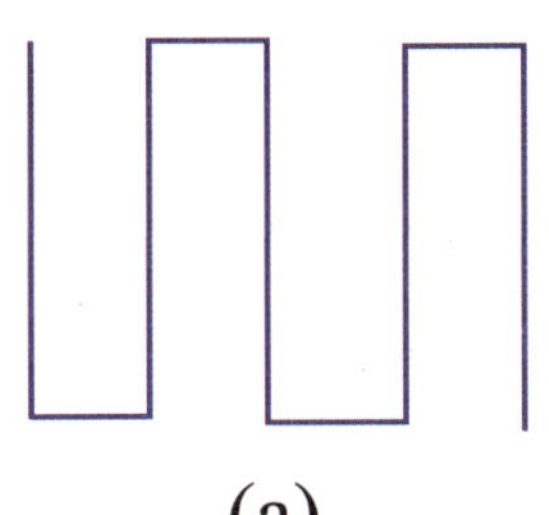
(a)

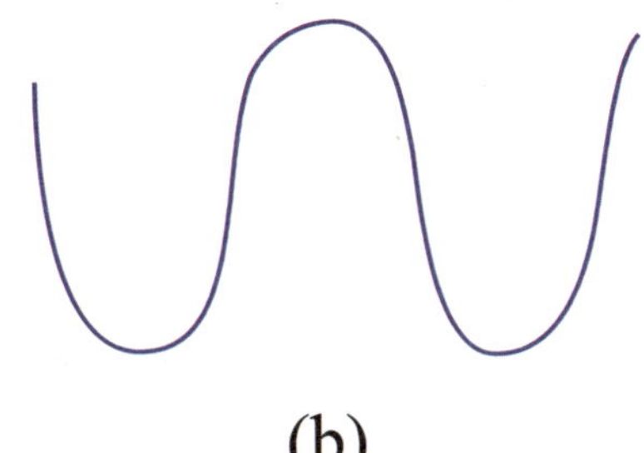
(b)

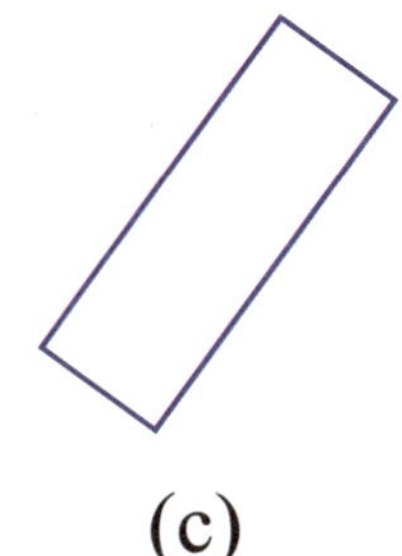
(c)

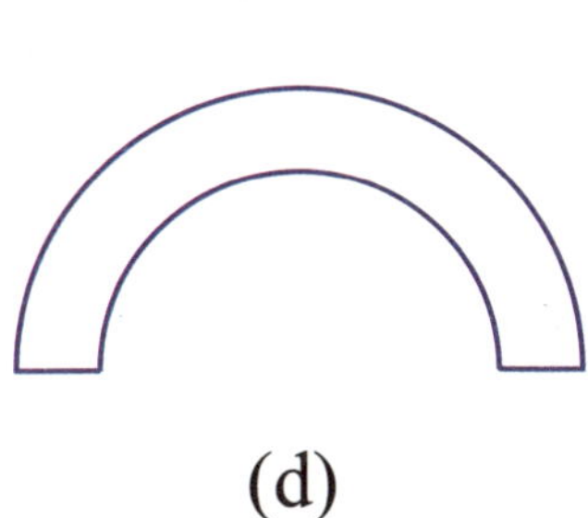
(d)

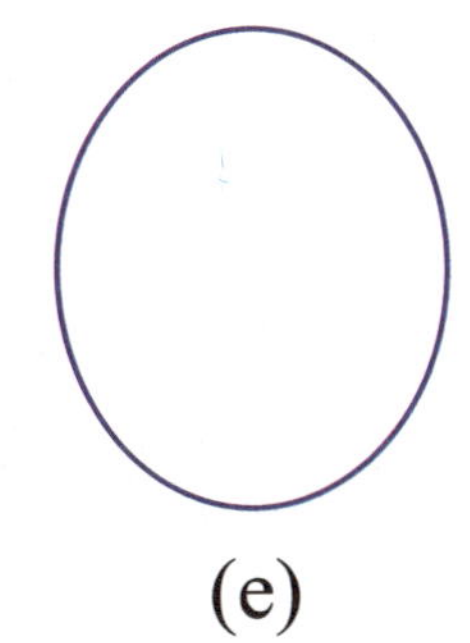
(e)

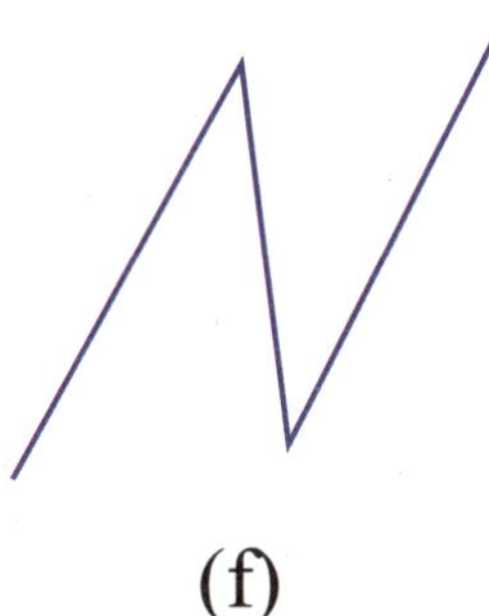
(f)

3. Fill in the blanks

a. A triangle has 3 ______ and ______ vertices.

b. A circle has ______ side and ______ vertex.

c. Every face of a ______ is a square.

d. In a ______ one face is plane and one face is curved.

e. A ______ has only one curved face and no edge and no corner.

4. Match the following

a.	Dice	Sphere	f.	Tetra pack of Juice
b.	Basket ball	Cylinder	g.	Ice cube
c.	Ice cream cone	cube	h.	Joker's cap
d.	Pencil	cone	i.	Book
e.	Chalk	Cuboid	j.	Match box

5. Give one word answer.
   a. A solid which has one face
   b. A solid which has one vertex
   c. A solid which has 3 faces, 2 edges and no vertex
6. Name any 3 objects which have
   a. Only flat surface
   b. Only curved surface
   c. Flat and curved surface

Mental Math

1. Fill in the blanks choosing the best option.
   a. A ________ has one face, no vertex (circle, sphere)
   b. A ________ has 6 faces, 12 edges, 8 vertices (cube, rectangle)
   c. A circle is a ________ figure (closed, open)
   d. Letter 'C' is a ________ figure (closed, open)
   e. Count the number of cubes in the following

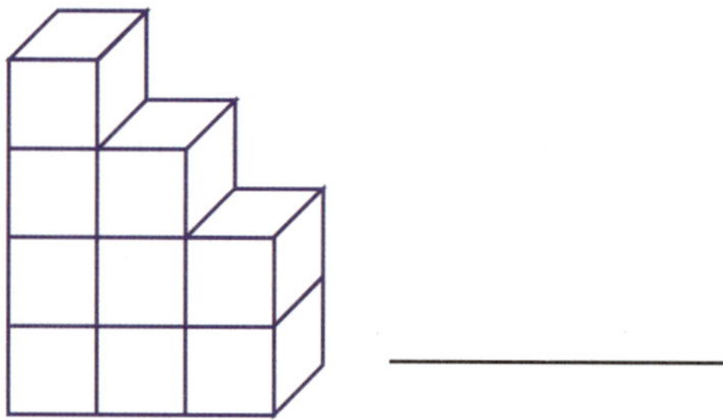

   f. Count and write the number of triangles in the following figure.

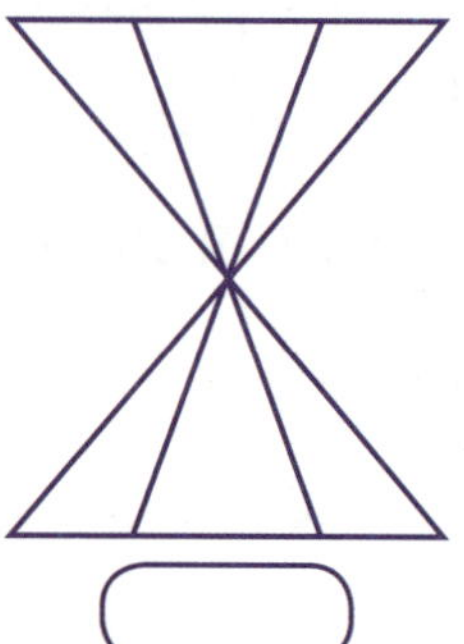

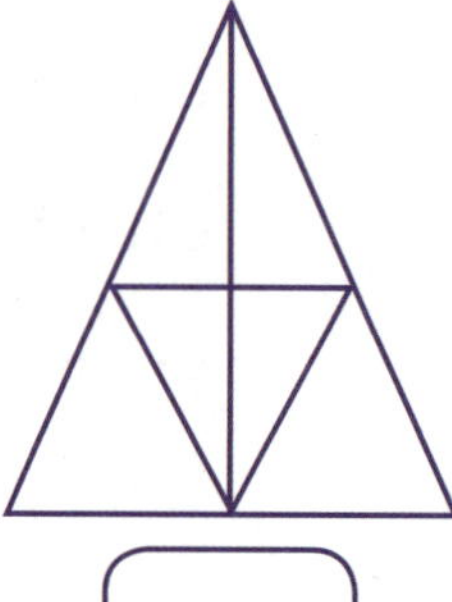

Data-Handling

15

Harry was fond of cars. One evening he sat outside his house and watched the cars that went past. He wanted to find out which was the most popular colour. He recorded his observation in the form of a table.

Colour	Tally Marks	Number
Red	~~IIII~~ ~~IIII~~ II	12
Blue	~~IIII~~ I	6
Black	~~IIII~~ IIII	9
Metallic Grey	~~IIII~~ III	8
White	~~IIII~~ ~~IIII~~ IIII	14
Yellow	I	1
		50

How did he record? Every time a car went by, he would put a '|' called a tally mark. His Mother told him after 4th, the 5th one should be a slash \ like this. It is like putting them in groups of 5.

Answer this

1. Which colour is least popular?

   Yellow

2. Which is most popular?

   White

He showed the table to his teacher. She appreciated it. She told him this could be done by another method, using pictures.

She took a situation where the students of a class were asked to tell the game each one likes to play.

2 children

A picture chart like this is called a pictograph.

1. How many children like tennis?

   ____

2. Which game is most popular?

   ____

3. Which two games are liked equally?

   ____

4. How many students are there in the class?

   ____

Exercise 15.1

1. Read the pictograph.

   Students present on a particular day

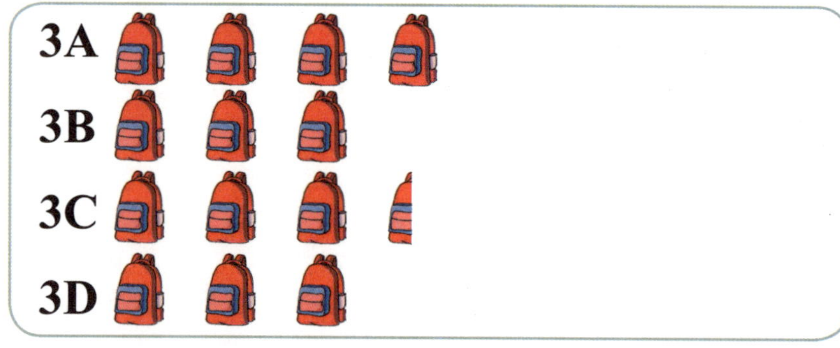

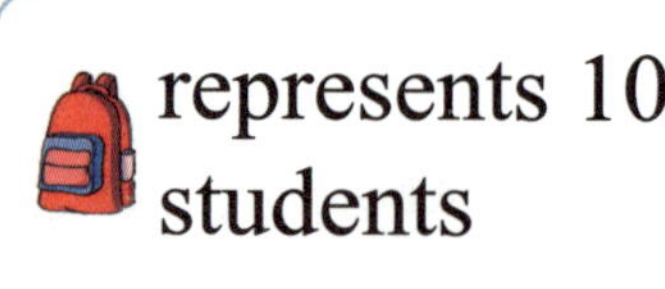
represents 10 students

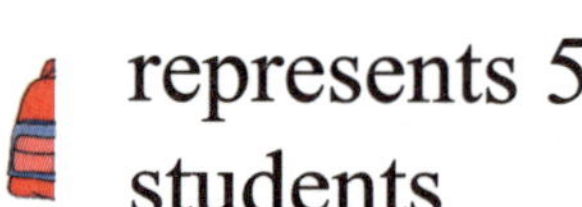
represents 5 students

Using this pictograph, answer the following questions.

a. Write the section with minimum attendance.

b. How many children were present on that day in class 3?

2. A survey conducted by Harry as like this

Favourite sandwich	Number of students
Cheese sandwich	13
Vegetable sandwich	6
Chicken sandwich	18
Egg sandwich	3

Show the above information in a table using tally marks.

3. A boy has a red ball, a black ball and a white ball. Some children recorded the results of drawing out a ball from the bag. The ball was put back in the bag after each draw.

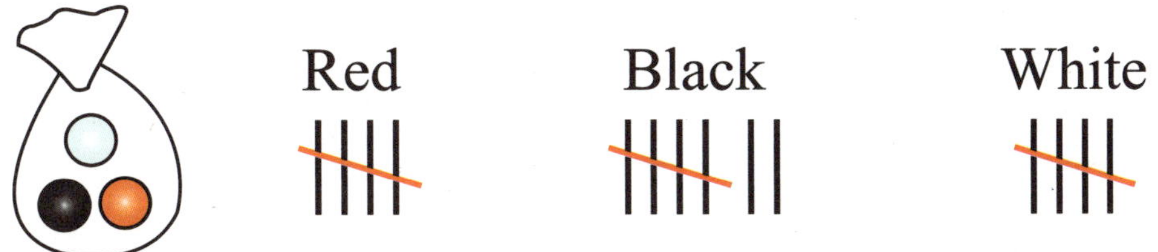

a. How many times was a ball drawn?

b. Which colour was drawn out least?

c. How many times was a red ball drawn?

d. What fraction of total was the white balls drawn?

4. Find the number of drinks in the refrigerator by filling up the table.

Drinks	Tally marks	Numbers
Coke	𝍸 𝍸	
Mango Juice		8
Lemonade	𝍸 𝍸 𝍷𝍷	
Orange Juice	𝍸 𝍸	
Apple Juice	𝍸 𝍸 𝍷𝍷𝍷𝍷	
Mountain dew	𝍸 𝍷𝍷𝍷𝍷	9

REVIEW EXERCISE 1

Based on 4-Digit Numbers, Addition, Subtraction

1. Write the numeral for
   a. Seven thousand and four ____________
   b. Two thousand and fifty six ____________
2. Write the number name for
   a. 4602 = ____________________
   b. 8001 = ____________________
3. Write in expanded form
   a. 5810 = ____________________
   b. 2015 = ____________________
4. Write the place value of the underlined digit.
   a. $42\underline{5}8$ ____________
   b. $29\underline{0}6$ ____________
   c. $\underline{7}693$ ____________
   d. $5\underline{7}14$ ____________
5. Form the greatest and smallest 4-digit number using the digits. 4, 6, 9, 8.
6. Find the missing numbers and fill in the boxes.
   a. 400 – ☐ = 263
   b. ☐ – 287 = 900
   c. 1203 + ☐ = 1827
   d. 2632 – ☐ = 840

7. Mrs. Francis has 3045 plants and Ms. Smith has 853 plants. Who has more plants and by how much?
8. For the Annual Day celebration 2468 children registered. Later 980 more children registered. But on the day of the celebration 1257 children did not turn up. How many attended the celebration?
9. Find the difference between the greatest 4-digit number and greatest 3-digit number.
10. Complete the pattern.

    2181, 2180, ________ ________ ________ ________

    9323, 9321, ________ ________ ________ ________

    7418, 7422, ________ ________ ________ ________

    1111, 1114, ________ ________ ________ ________

    4000, 4011, ________ ________ ________ ________
11. Find the sum of all odd numbers between 624 and 630
12. Write all the even numbers between 1985 and 2011.

PUZZLE TIME

1. Find two numbers such that their sum is 9 and difference is also 9.
2. There are 63 steps of a monument. Harry is standing in the middle, he has _______ steps to walk up or _______ steps to walk down.
3. Which step is he standing on? _______

REVIEW EXERCISE 2

Based on Multipication Division

1. Complete the following

   a. $7 + 7 + 7 + 7 = 7 \times$ ☐ b. $8 \times$ ☐ $= 8$

   c. ☐ $\times 16 = 0$ d. $2 \times 500 =$ ☐

   e. $3 \times 700 =$ ☐ $\times 3$ f. $17 \times 21 = 357$, then $357 \div 21 =$ ☐

   g. $468 \times 700 \times 0 =$ ☐ h. $780 \div 10 =$ ☐

   i. $20 \times 10 =$ ☐ $\times 100$

2. How many centuries form 7000? ☐

3. Find the product

   a. 123×96

   b. 209×5

4. Find the quotient and remainder

   a. $768 \div 9$

   b. $1245 \div 5$

5. Product of 2 numbers is 273. If one is 7 find the other.

6. Multiply & complete the grid.

×	13	24	17	32	40
2	26				
4				128	
6			102		
10					

7. Fill in the blanks and colour according to the key given below.

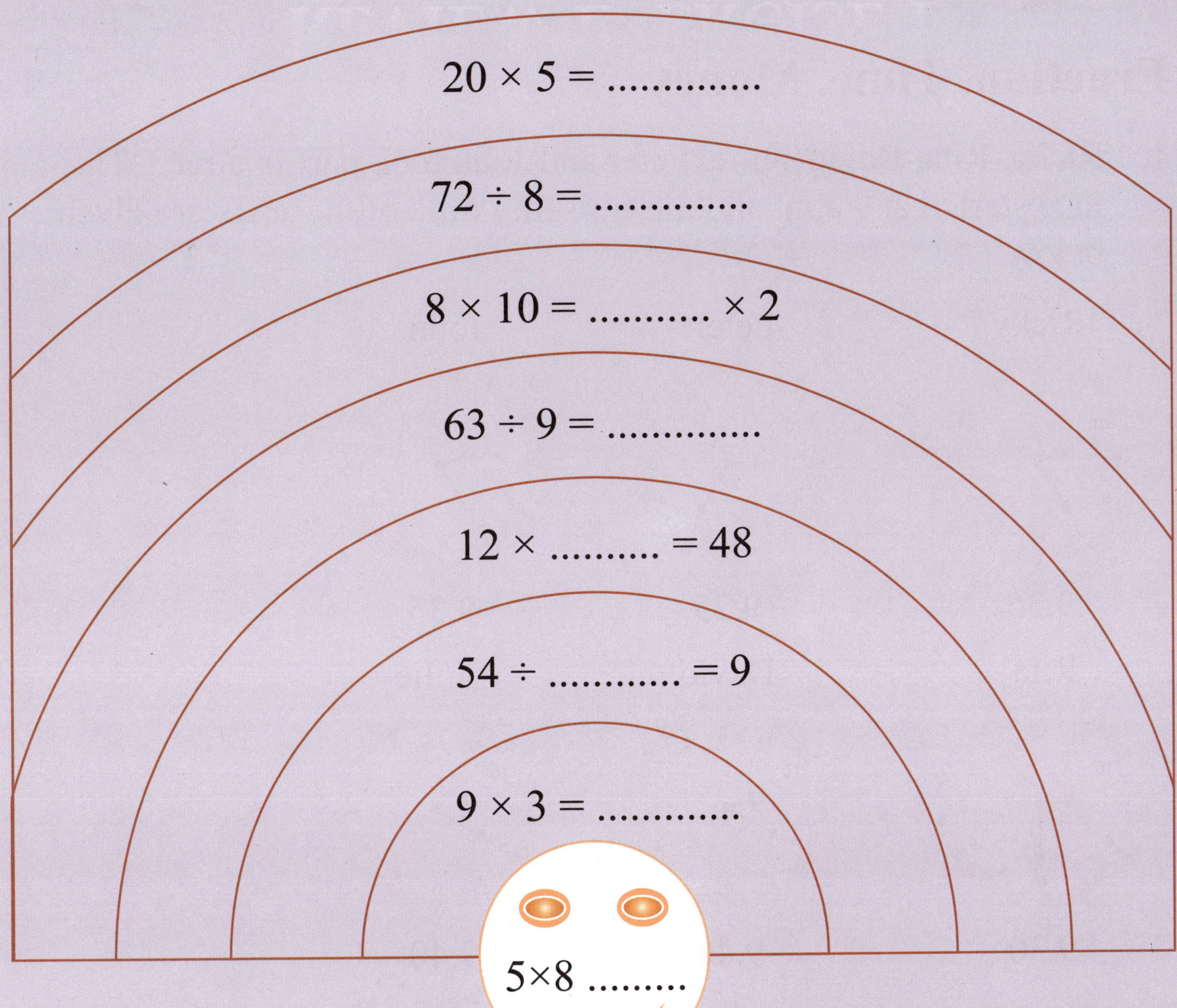

Light blue	4	Yellow	40
Red	100	Green	7
Pink	18	Blue	13
Orange	9	Violet	27
Grey	12	Indigo	6

REVIEW EXERCISE 3

Fraction, Time, Money

1. Ricky, Rita, David, Julie, Peter and John took part in a race. The race started at 9 a.m. and the finishing time of these six are given below:

Now answer the following

a. Who won the race?

b. Who stood last?

c. How long did David and Julie take to finish the race?

d. Did anyone take more than 40 minutes?

2. Cross out whichever is incorrect. Time taken to

a. make a phone call 5 mins / 5 hours

b. sleep at night 8 hours / 8 mins

c. watch T.V. 1 min / 1 hour

d. study 2 mins / 2 hours

e. eat breakfast 10 mins / 10 seconds

3. Match the fraction with its correct name

a.	$\frac{1}{2}$	i) three-fourths
b.	$\frac{1}{3}$	ii) two-fifths
c.	$\frac{3}{4}$	iii) five-eights
d.	$\frac{2}{5}$	iv) half
e.	$\frac{5}{8}$	v) one-third

4. Fill in the blanks

a. If an apple costs \$ 10, an orange costs \$ 6 and a banana costs \$ 5, the total cost of 5 apple, 4 oranges and 3 bananas is ______.

b. Julie was born on 20 October, 2004. David is 9 months younger to her. David was born in

i. July 2004 ii. July 2005 iii. Jan 2004 iv. Aug 2005

c. A man saves \$ 60 per week. He saves \$ ______ everday.

i. \$ 8.58 ii. \$ 9.60 iii. \$ 10 iv. \$ 11.36

d. 75 ¢ is

i. \$ 7.50 ii. \$ 0.75 iii. \$ 7.05 iv. \$ 75

REVIEW EXERCISE 4

Geometry, Length, Mass-capacity, Data-Handling

1. The length of a rectangular room is 20 m and its breadth is 10 m 50 cm less. Find the breadth of the room.
2. A child weighs 8 kg 800 g. After 4 months he has gained 2 kg 250 g. Find his new weight.
3. Tom is 1 m 4 cm tall and his sister is shorter by 6 cm. How tall is his sister?
4. My mother buys 2 L of Olive oil every month. Our monthly consumption is 850 mL. How much of oil is left?
5. A box full of books weighs 46 kg 850 g. The weight of the empty box is 3 kg 50 g. Find the weight of the books in the box.
6. A man buys 35 L of petrol and puts 10 L 425 mL in his bike and 18 L 750 mL in his car. How much petrol is left with him?
7. The picture shows collection of books in a library on different subjects.

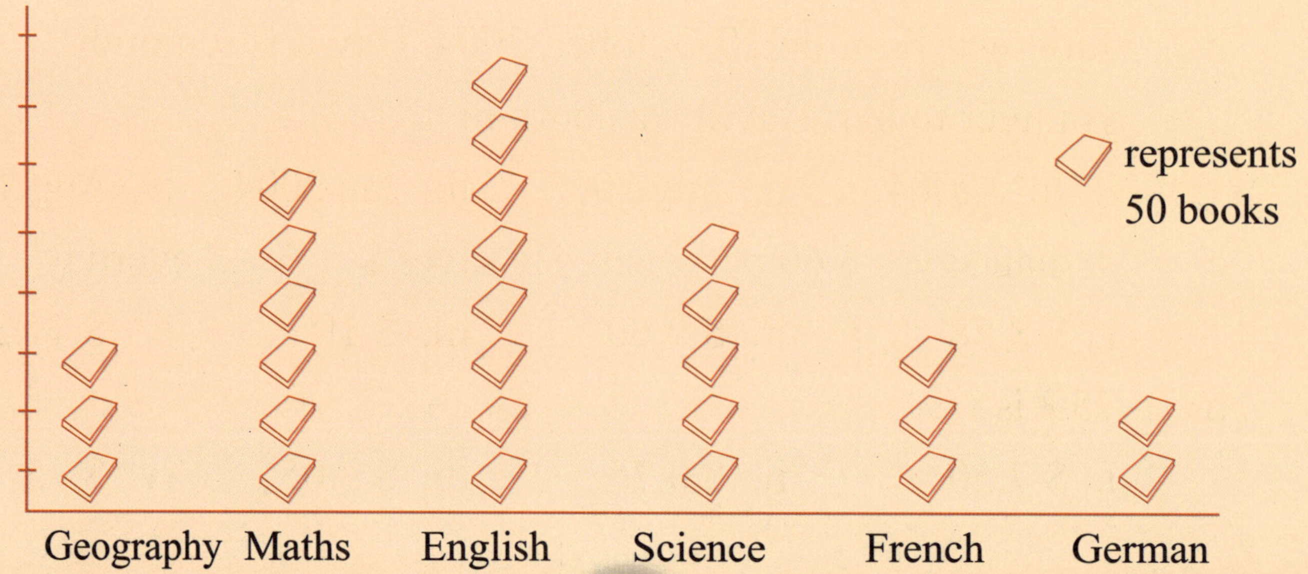

Answer the questions

a. How many Geography books are there?

b. Which subject has the minimum number of books?

c. How many Maths books are there?

d. Which subjects have the same number of books?

e. What is the total number of books?

Answers

CHAPTER 2

Exercises 2.1

1. a. 5105 b. 7002 c. 4320 d. 7257
   e. 2010 f. 1063
3. a. 6606 b. 5050 c. 1022 d. 4004
   e. 9579 f. 8008 g. 4340

Exercises 2.2

1. a. 6000 + 800 + 50 + 4
   b. 3000 + 700 + 0 + 1
   c. 9000 + 100 + 90 + 0
   d. 2000 + 500 + 0 + 8
   e. 5000 + 200 + 70 + 3
   f. 4000 + 0 + 40 + 4
2. a. 3700 b. 1066 c. 4102 d. 6010
   e. 9005 f. 5050 g. 7076 h. 8808
3. a. 1001 b. 4990 c. 3010 d. 2679
   e. 6000 f. 2751
4. a. 2679 b. 4000 c. 7999 d. 5209
   e. 999 f. 3099
5. a. 4089, 4091
   b. 3099, 3101
   c. 6153, 6155

d. 5998, 6000

e. 1389, 1391

f. 2008, 2010

Exercises 2.3

1. a. 9801 b. 3303 c. 5768 d. 1101

   e. 2076 f. 8806 g. 6002

2. a. 6000 b. 700 c. 0 d. 80

   e. 1 f. 0

3. a. 2376, 2378, 2380, 2382, 2384

   b. 6597, 6599, 6601, 6603, 6605

   c. 4008, 4010, 4012, 4014, 4016

4. a. 2880, 2890, 2900, 2910, 2920

   b. 6367, 6377, 6387, 6397, 6407

   c. 4502, 4512, 4522, 4532, 4542

5. a. 5790, 5890, 5990, 6090, 6190

   b. 2988, 3088, 3188, 3288, 3388 c. 6701, 6801, 6901, 7001, 7101

6. a. 7101, 7103, 7105, 7107, 7109

   b. 4006, 4016, 4026, 4036, 4046

   c. 5805, 5905, 6005, 6105, 6205

   d. 2330, 2329, 2328, 2327, 2326

Exercises 2.4

1. a. < b. < c. < d. >

   e. > f. >

2. a. 3729, 3725, 3724, 3721

   b. 4689, 4680, 4674, 4605

   c. 5102, 5012, 2105, 2015

3. a. 1234, 4132, 4231, 4321
   b. 4067, 4076, 5067, 6057
   c. 81, 810, 1080, 3010
4. a. 408, 406, 640, 840
   b. 8064, 8604, 8460, 6840
5. b. 9730, 3079
   c. 8410, 1048
   d. 6550, 5056
   e. 4321, 1234
   f. 7641, 1467

Exercises 2.5

1. a. 1 b. 2 c. 3 d. 4 e. 9
2. a. XI b. XII c. XIII d. XIV
   e. XVII f. XVIII g. XIX h. XX
3. a. XI b. XII c. VIII d. XXIV
   e. XXVIII
4. a. XIV b. VII c. XXIX d. XXXV
   e. XXXI f. XV
5. a. 39 b. 18 c. 13 d. 34
   e. 26 f. 14
6. a. × b. × c. ✓ d. ×
   e. × f. ✓

CHAPTER 3

Exercises 3.1

1. b. Twelve thousand three hundred nine

c. Ten thousand six hundred seventy one

d. Two thousand eighty two

e. Six thousand forty five

f. Four thousand four hundred one

g. Three thousand five hundred and three

h. Six thousand three hundred ten

i. Three thousand four hundred eighty

j. Nine thousand four hundred thirty three

Exercises 3.2

a. 4 T + 3 O = 43

b. 25 T + 5 O = 2 H +5 T + 5 O=255

c. 13 T + 7 O = 137

d. 3 H 4 T 6 O = 346

e. 17 T 8 O = 178

f. 10 H 8 T 3 O = 1083

g. 1 TH 2 H + 3 H + 4 T = 1540

h. 7 H 4 H 5 T = 1150

Exercises 3.3

1. a. 7 T 17 O =8 T 7 O = 87

   b. 7 T 13 O = 8 T 3 O = 83

   c. 3 H 3 T 13 O = 3H 4T 3O = 343

   d. 3 H 9 T 7 O = 397

2. a. 7245 + 1431 = 8676

   b. 2521 + 3769 = 6290

   c. 167 + 55 = 222

   d. 1974 + 3897 = 5871

   e. 5432 + 3341 = 8773

   f. 3512 + 2745 = 6257

Exercises 3.4

1. a. 8226 tickets

   b. 8841 clips

   c. 5050 books

   d. 9726 people

   e. 14125 km

Mental Maths

a. 1

b. 10

c. 20

d. 2000

e. 300

f. 1090 g. 1364 h. 1227 i. 2000 j. 1000

k. 3264 l. 2073 m. 525 n. 6013 o. 4510

CHAPTER 4

Exercises 4.1

1. a. 241 b. 234 c. 160 d. 115

Exercises 4.2

1. a. 2222 b. 3030 c. 1001 d. 3223
   e. 1220 f. 1111 g. 1110 h. 2141

Exercises 4.3

1. a. 1856 b. 3273 c. 1023 d. 2462
   e. 2563 f. 1105 g. 1995 h. 2505
2. a. 4,3 b. 8,4 c. 2,6,0,0,1 d. 2,5,8

Exercises 4.4

a. 1517 b. 2868 c. 2855 d. 3792 e. 625 f. 6450

Exercises 4.5

1. a. 4232 b. 728 c. 3756 d. 1566 e. 2281
2. a. 232 b. 1798 c. 1809

Mental Maths

1.

a. 0 b. 55 c. 54 d. 901 e. 47 f. 0

g. 26 h. 500 i. 14 j. 1 k. 40

CHAPTER 5

Exercises 5.1

a. $2 \times 9 = 18$ b. $3 \times 8 = 24$ c. $5 \times 6 = 30$

d. $4 \times 10 = 40$ e. $6 \times 4 = 24$ f. $7 \times 3 = 21$

g. $3 \times 2 = 6$ h. $5 \times 5 = 25$ i. $3 \times 11 = 33$

j. $5 \times 7 = 35$ k. $3 \times 12 = 36$

Exercises 5.2

1. a. 7 b. 0 c. 16 d. 5000 e. 87
   f. 617;418 g. 999 h. 0 i. 121

Exercises 5.3

1. a. 68 b. 84 c. 88 d. 69
   e. 99 f. 268 g. 312 h. 888
   i. 609 j. 1284 k. 219 l. 2408
   m. 1236 n. 1408 o. 2092

2. a. 228 b. 192 c. 304 d. 170
   e. 203 f. 720 g. 168 h. 306
   i. 175 j. 462

3. a. 1136 b. 940 c. 927 d. 632
   e. 1869 f. 1152 g. 834 h. 3216
   i. 5872 j. 5121

Exercises 5.4

1. a. 300 b. 2690 c. 8600 d. 1000

e. 7800 f. 87300

2. a. 3700 b. 1 c. 490 d. 100
   e. 100 f. 0 g. 100 h. 90

Exercises 5.5

1. a. 680 b. 510 c. 9600 d. 6500 e. 6440
   f. 4800 g. 1680 h. 9000 i. 3200 j. 1000
   k. 4800 l. 3250 m. 3000 n. 5000

2. a. $ 40 b. 300 pins c. 240 hours d. 63 hours
   e. 1250 lines f. 3300 bags

Exercises 5.6

1. b. $18 \times 17 = 18 \times (10 + 7) = 18 \times 10 + 18 \times 7 = 180 + 126 = 306$
   c. $19 \times 23 = 19 \times (20+3) = 19 \times 20 + 19 \times 3 = 380 + 57 = 427$
   d. $22 \times 11 = 22 \times (10+1) = 22 \times 10 + 22 \times 1 = 220 + 22 = 242$

Exercises 5.7

1. a. 874 b. 2548 c. 4256 d. 2880 e. 4224 f. 1463
   g. 3255 h. 9828 i. 7514 j. 9633 k. 2352 l. 6560
   m. 6084 n. 8650 o. 6768

Exercises 5.8

1. a. 5775 toys b. 3654 flats c. 7608 crayons d. 9350 sentences
   e. 1700 trees f. 2610 books g. 1496 seats h. 4092 cycles

Mental Maths

1. a. 0 b. 1 c. 72 d. 4×9 e. 15 f. 3200

g. 50 h. 1000 i. 490 j. 24 k. 100 l. 120

m. $ 100

CHAPTER 6

Exercises 6.1

1. a. 6 , 3 b. 2 , 5 c. 4 , 4 d. 30 , 30

2. a. 3 b. 10 c. 8 d. 3 e. 4
f. 2 g. 6 h. 3 i. 7 j. 3
k. 7 l. 42 m. 3

3. a. 7 b. 3 c. 18 d. 9 e. 6
f. 10 g. 4 h. 9 i. 9 j. 50
k. 5 l. 30 m. 6 n. 8 o. 0

4. b. $12 \div 2 = 6$ $12 \div 6 = 2$ c. $18 \div 2 = 9$ $18 \div 9 = 2$
d. $20 \div 10 = 2$ $20 \div 2 = 10$ e. $40 \div 5 = 8$ $40 \div 8 = 5$
f. $36 \div 4 = 9$ $36 \div 9 = 4$ g. $35 \div 7 = 5$ $35 \div 5 = 7$
h. $63 \div 9 = 7$ $63 \div 7 = 9$ i. $72 \div 8 = 9$ $72 \div 9 = 8$

Exercises 6.2

1. a. 6 b. 3 c. 8 d. 7 e. 7
f. 6 g. 6 h. 7 i. 9

Exercises 6.3

a. 24 b. 11 c. 43 d. 21 e. 22 f. 11
g. 32 h. 34 i. 31 j. 10 k. 23 l. 11

Exercises 6.4

1. a. Q=23 R=2 b. Q=17 R=1 c. Q=19 R=0 d. Q=16
R=4 e. Q=12 R=4 f. Q=13 R=0 g. Q=14
R=0 h. Q=24 R=2 i. Q=17 R=0 j. Q=13
R=1 k. Q=12 R=3 l. Q=15 R=4

Exercises 6.5

1. a. 219 b. 10 c. 99 d. 74 e. 98 f. 171
   g. 73 h. 95 i. 91 j. 14 k. 99 l. 45

Exercises 6.6

1. a. 321 b. 89,3 c. 82,0 d. 141,2 e. 66,4
   f. 255,0 g. 220,0 h. 261,1 i. 50,6 j. 51,8
   k. 100,0 l. 134,3 m. 16,4 n. 90,4 o. 39,2
   p. 64,1 q. 155,0 r. 91,2 s. 91,4 t. 79,5
   u. 109

2. a. 7,8 b. 44,4 c. 93,5 d. 21,9 e. 343,8
   f. 777,7 g. 83,3 h. 706 i. 10,7

Exercises 6.7

1. a. 8,2 b. 251 c. 752 d. 230
   e. 560 weeks f. 60 benches g. 272 toys h. 708
   i. 9 hours j. 68 trees

Mental Maths

1. a. $28 + 7 = 35 \div 5 = 7 \times 7 = 49 - 7 = 42$
   b. $5 + 5 = 10 \times 5 = 50 \div 5 = 10 - 5 = 5$
   c. $64 \div 8 = 8 \times 9 = 72 + 3 = 75 - 20 = 55$

d. $3 \times 10 = 30 \div 5 = 6 + 16 = 22 - 2 = 20$

IN	OUT
90	810
22	198
1	9
7	63
10	90

IN	OUT
41	369
500	4500
31	279
2	18
10	90

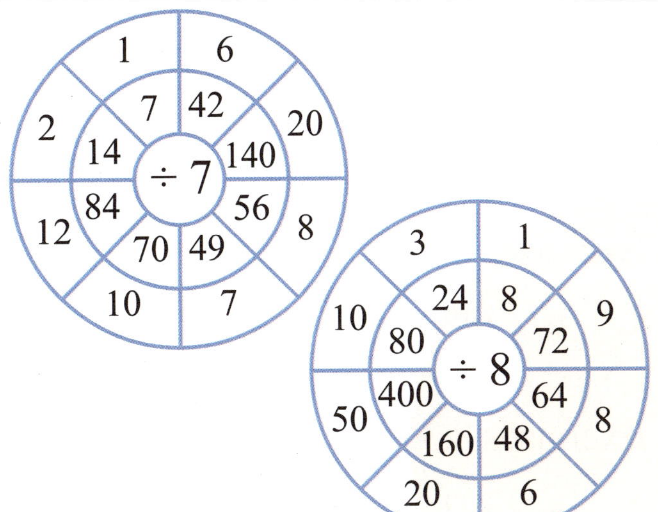

CHAPTER 7

Exercises 7.3

1.

	Fraction	number	denominator	name
a.	4/7	4	7	four-sevenths
b.	2/3	2	3	two-third
c.	13/20	13	20	thirteen-twentieth
d.	3/8	3	8	three-eighths
e.	8/11	8	11	eight-elevenths

3. a. $\frac{2}{3}$ b. $\frac{4}{6}$ c. $\frac{3}{5}$

5. a. 1/4 b. 5/10 c. 5/8 d. 4/25 e. 6/12 f. 3/8

Mental Maths

1. numerator, denominator

2. 3/7

3. fraction, 4/5

CHAPTER 8

Exercises 8.1

1. a. 4:00 b. 10:00 c. 8:00 d. 11:00

Exercises 8.2

1. a. 9:30 b. 2:30 c. 1:30 d. 6:30

Exercises 8.3

1. a. 4:15 b. 12:15 c. 9:15 d. 10:15
   e. 5:15 f. 1:15 g. 7:15 h. 3:15

Exercises 8.4

1. a. 240 b. 72 c. 480 d. 168 e. 216 f. 168
2. a. 300 b. 1200 c. 900 d. 480 e. 1440 f. 720
3. a. 21 b. 19
4. a. F b. F c. F

Exercises 8.5

1. a. 56 b. 28 c. 180 d. 70 e. 90 f. 300

2. 1. Labour day 2. Teacher's day 3. American Independence day
   4. Nelson Mandela's birthday 5. Universal Children's day 6. Christmas

3. 5th July

4. 1999

Mental Maths

1. 6:45 2. 14 3. Tuesday 4. Friday 5. Tuesday
6. 8:05 7. 19 8. 15 9. 5 10. 3

CHAPTER 9

Exercises 9.1

a, c. e, f,

CHAPTER 10

Exercises 10.1

2. a. 8000 b. 1300 c. 7070 d. 12500 e. 1804 f. 90
   g. 2125 h. 5600

3. a. 3.75 b. 20.15 c. 10.01 d. 30 e. 6.80 f. 9.90
   g. 12 h. 60.75 i. 72.10

Exercises 10.2

1. a. $ 97.23 b. 133.10 c. 1211.64 d. 246.23 e. 228.85
   f. 1436.97 g. 584.60 h. 364.37 i. 785.75 j. 1444.43
   k. 2021.00 l. 898.80

2. a. $ 236.50 b. 1101.30 c. 1189.85 d. 1363 e. 92.10

3. a. $ 10.07 b. 52.29 c. 59.49 d. 457.75

4. a. $ 1.25 b. 266.67 c. 64.10 d. 0.20 e. 2.40

Exercises 10.3

1. 21 2. 35.50 3. 73.70 4. 25.00
5. 28.75 6. 5 7. 2.10 8. 34.40

Mental Maths

1. 65 2. 4.25 3. 7000 4. 90 5. 13 6. 10.05
7. 44.75 8. > 9. = 10. 10

CHAPTER 11

Exercises 11.1

1. a. 6000 b. 3950 c. 8450 d. 7225

2. a. 800 b. 370 c. 1000 d. 910 e. 600 f. 775

3. a. 1000 b. 100 c. 3000 d. 10 e. 10; 25

Exercises 11.2

1. a. 6 b. 9 m 25 cm c. 10 d. 1 m 50 cm e. 6000
   f. 7000 g. 3000 h. 8000 + 880 = 8880

Exercises 11.3

1. a. 64 m 60 cm b. 99 m 34 cm c. 215 m 95 cm d. 181 m 57 cm
   e. 122 m 48 cm
2. a. 144 m 33 cm b. 176 m 57 cm c. 2 m 60 cm d. 47 m 47 cm
3. 49 cm

4. Mohan 135 cm

5. 700 m

CHAPTER 12

Exercises 12.1

1. a. 70 g b. 1 kg c. 800 g d. 3 g e. 50 g f. 70 kg

Exercises 12.2

1. b. $5 \times 1000 = 5000$ g c. $7 \times 1000 = 7000$ g d. $5000 + 800 = 5800$ g
   e. $3 \times 1000 + 215 = 3215$ g f. $6000 + 495 = 6495$ g g. $8000 + 8 = 8008$
   h. $3000 + 30 = 3030$ g

Exercises 12.3

1. a. 8 kg b. 5 kg 895 g c. 2 kg 900 g d. 6 kg 75 g
   e. 3 kg 365 g
2. a. 13 kg 500 g b. 27 kg 925 g c. 4 kg 415 g d. 25 kg 775 g
   e. 30 g
3. a. $>$ b. $>$ c. $<$ d. $>$
   e. $<$ f. $=$ g. $>$ h. $>$
4. a. 8 kg 750 g b. 3 kg 900 g c. 44 kg 500 g d. 36 kg 250 g
   e. 18 kg 650 g

CHAPTER 13

Exercises 13.1

1. a. mL b. L c. mL d. mL
   e. mL f. L g. mL

2. a. 20 mL b. 500 mL c. 5 mL

Exercises 13.2

1. b. 8 L 125 mL= 8 × 1000 mL+ 125 mL= 8000 mL+ 25 mL= 8125 mL
   c. 7 L 555 mL= 7 × 1000 mL+ 555 mL= 7000 mL+ 555 mL= 7555 mL
   d. 4 L 28 mL= 4000 mL+ 28 mL= 4028 mL
   e. 3 L 15 mL= 3015 mL
2. a. 7 b. 8 c. 6 L 500 mL d. 2 L 850 mL
   e. 1 L 95 mL f. 6 L 80 mL g. 9 L 590 mL
3. a. 4000 b. 6 c. 750 d. 7354
   e. 5 L 50 mL f. 9 g. 6 L 375 mL h. L

Exercises 13.3

1. a. 42 L 742 mL b. 84 L 380 mL c. 51 L 847 mL d. 79 L 56 mL
   e. 85 L 196 mL f. 68 L 239 mL
2. a. 2 L 800 mL b. 9 L 500 mL c. 11 L 873 mL d. 22 L 923 mL
   e. 11 L 586 mL
3. a. 2 L 120 mL b. 75 L 930 mL c. 1 L 30 mL d. 5 L 250 mL

Mental Maths

1. 45.38 2. 4 3. L or mL 4. 7000 5. 4 kg 950 g
6. 9.50 7. 4 8. 135, 116 9. a. cm b. g
c. L d. m e. km f. mL

CHAPTER 14

Exercises 14.1

1. a. cone, cylinder b. cuboid, cylinder c. cone, cylinder
   d. curved e. plane, curved

2. a. orange b. a circular wall clock

Exercises 14.2

1. a. square b. triangle c. rectangle d. circle

2 a. open b. open c. closed d. closed e. closed f. open

3. a. 3 sides, 3 b. no, no c. book d. vase e. ball

4. a. cube b. sphere c. cone d. cylinder
   e. cube f. cuboid g. cube h. cone

5. a. ball b. ice cream cone

6. a. book, duster, pencil box b. egg, orange, apple
   c. water bottle, glass

Mental Maths

1. 1. sphere 2. cube 3. closed 4. open 5. 9 6. 12 ;9

CHAPTER 15

Exercises 15.1

1. a. B,D b. 135
3. a. 17
   b. RED, WHITE
   c. 5
   d. 5/17
4. 10 8 12 10 14 9

Review Exercise 1

1. a. 7004 b. 2056
2. a. Four thousand six hundred and two b. Eight thousand one
3. a. 5000+800+10 b. 2000+10+5
4. a. 50 b. 0 c. 7000 d. 700
5. 9864 , 4689
6. a. 137 b. 1187 c. 624 d. 1792
7. Mrs. Francis , 2192
8. 2191
9. 9000
10. 2179, 2178, 2177, 2176 9319, 9317, 9315 7426, 7430, 7434, 7438
    1117, 1120, 1123.1127 4022, 4033, 4044, 4055
11. 1881
12. 1986, 1988, 1990, 1992, 1994, 1996, 1998, 2000

Puzzle Time

1. 0,9 2. 31,31 3. 32

Review Exercise 2

1. a. 4 b. 1 c. 9 d. 1000 e. 700
   f. 17 g. 0 h. 78 i. 2
2. 70
3. a. 11808 b. 1045
4. a. 85.3 b. 249
5. 39

Review Exercise 3

2. a. 5 mins b. 8 hours c. 1 hour d. 2 hours e. 10 mins
3. a. iv b. v c. i d. ii e. iii
4. a. 89 b. ii c. i d. ii

Review Exercise 4

1. 9 m 50 cm 2. 11 kg 50 g 3. 98 cm 4. 1 L 150 mL
5. 43 kg 800 g 6. 5 L 825 mL
7. a. 150 b. German c. 300 d. Geography, French e. 1350